# DANCING
# ON THIN ICE

*By the same author*

In Liberal Doses
Telling It Straight

# DANCING ON THIN ICE

## MARINA MAHATHIR

To Ani,

Hot off the press, my latest tome! May all the work we do lead to the world we want for our kids — progressive, just and peaceful!

love
Marina
21/11/15

**edm** EDITIONS
DIDIER
MILLET

AUTHOR'S ACKNOWLEDGEMENTS
I would like to thank Editions Didier Millet especially Martin Cross
for not allowing me to wait another 11 years before I do another book.
I would also like to thank my editors at *The Star*, Santha Oorjitham,
Soo Ewe Jin as well as Dato' Seri Wong Chun Wai, for their patience at
my various rants, and my editors at *Nanyang Siang Pao* who translate
my columns into Mandarin.

And I would especially like to thank my readers who accost me
everywhere, camera phone in hand, to tell me they love my column,
blog, postings and anything else I write (some of which may not even
have been written by me!). I am grateful always for their support
without which I may have fallen through the ice a long time ago.

To my daughters Ineza and Shasha who are blossoming
into feisty young fighters for all that is right and good,

To my father whose genetic spirit flows
through their veins and mine,

To my mother, whose sweetness and gentleness
never fails to temper us,

And to my husband Tara
who has put up with all our sass with such patience.

Love you all.

The contents of this book first appeared in *The Star**.
Read more Musings by Marina Mahathir every fortnight
in *The Star*.

*with the exception of the articles marked with an asterisk in the Contents.

# Contents

# Supporting the Good, Shaming the Bad

Marina Mahathir is tireless! How she can write her column, without fail, for over 20 years, I cannot fathom. While I struggle to produce one column a month, she makes it seem effortless. Her wit, sarcasm and eye-rolling bewilderment at the stupidities of those in power constitute therapy for her legions of fans.

While the children of powerful people usually keep their opinions to themselves, Marina fearlessly gives voice to those who are disempowered, marginalised and persecuted, and gives hell to those in power. She calls a spade a spade, and that must make many a public figure squirm in discomfort, if not annoyance and even anger.

What I admire most in Marina, as a person and a writer, is the courage of her convictions – a scarce commodity among the leaders of our nation. She takes on causes of those most marginalised in society. She put HIV/AIDs on the front-burner of public health, helped to destigmatise the issue, made it safe for corporations to donate millions to the cause, and cool for politicians and society leaders to champion it. She even made a conscious effort to improve her Bahasa Malaysia, and build on the specialised vocabulary of the subject matter so that she can speak and write on it in order to reach the community most affected by it.

When a certain persistently obnoxious politician formed an anti-homosexual group, she was the first to publicly condemn him and his hate campaign against citizens who already suffer prejudice and discrimination for their sexual orientation.

Her biting sarcasm in pointing out the shameless hypocrisy of politicians and officials never fails to bring chuckles whenever I read her column. Who could disagree when she berated the Immigration official who accused a Malaysian transsexual facing deportation from the UK of bringing 'shame' to the country, and yet never accused the more than 30,000 Malaysians who had overstayed of the same offence to national pride.

You will often find Marina listing in her columns other incidents of 'shaming' Malaysia that seem to occur regularly but for which the culprits are not hung out to dry. Like the numerous times when government delegates at international conferences disappear and return later with bags full of shopping; or when they have absolutely nothing to say at a meeting, and NGOs with expertise on the subject matter come to their rescue; or when they say patently untrue things and expound on theories with no empirical evidence at a press conference and you hold your tongue because you don't want to, ahem, 'shame' them in front of the world press. And yet, as she writes in her column 'Oh, the Shame of it All', it is 'NGOs who know their stuff who get told off for being disloyal, unpatriotic and supposedly out to embarrass the government.'

Marina's writings on religion and women's rights are trenchant. She calls out the intolerance, bigotry and narrow-mindedness of those who proclaim themselves to be doing things for God when they are simply doing them for personal gain. She is tireless in pointing out there are far more important things to worry about than what one wears or drinks or 'whether rooms can be used for one faith or another, or what one calls God or whether everyone fits into one uniform faith box or not.'

She calls out the men and women in leadership position who blithely say we don't need a women's rights movement in Malaysia because women were granted equality, including the right to vote from the start. As she has said, tell that to the single mothers fighting for their rights in the courts, to the women who remain legally married but in reality have no spouses, and to the women bypassed for promotion by less-qualified men.

Marina speaks out because these things need to be said, aloud. Thus, the ever-growing fanbase of tens of thousands following her every word on Facebook and Twitter. Which makes her a powerful and influential voice for change. Thank God. For, more than anything else, Marina is an indefatigable bridge-builder at a time when the country is more polarised than ever, with a leadership that remains silent as hate speeches bellow from desperate politicians and their minions. She lends her name, her presence and her influence to all those who want to do good, whether it is to  celebrate our diversity or to heal the wounds.

While into my sixth decade, I can't wait to be a lazy bum, Marina is still brimming with ideas, new ways of doing things, lending support to yet more causes and events, organised by the young, the discriminated, and the marginalised, helping to right what is wrong.

Just as she writes tirelessly to share her views, values and convictions, she also follows through with deeds to match. It is citizens like Marina who give many of us hope that all is not lost with Malaysia.

Zainah Anwar
*October 2015*

# Reflecting on the Busy Year That Was

It's the end of the year, folks and a good time to sit and review the 365 days gone past. For me it has been an exhausting one with so much work and things happening all the time. I talked and talked and talked, to women's groups, academics and students and anyone else who's interested, both here and abroad. I joined the 150,000 or so Malaysians who marched at Bersih 3.0 and was shocked that such a peaceful march could have been so badly distorted in the media. I got a new book out and did several book signings at various bookstores and got the opportunity to meet the people who actually read me.

I feel like I've had more things inputted into the hard disk in my head than any time before. One can never stop learning, I found out, and to grow, we need to cast aside our preconceptions and prejudices first. Only then can our minds be free to accept new knowledge.

What is the purpose of that knowledge? To me it can only be to serve others, in my country and the world. In a time when knowledge is power, and those who have knowledge try and keep it to themselves, or worse, distort for their own ends, more than ever we need to do everything we can to democratise knowledge. Equality only comes when knowledge is shared so that power can be shared.

Some of us are lucky and privileged to have access to new knowledge all the time. I count myself as one of them, and I find my most scintillating bouts of learning when I am among women. Women seek knowledge to find solutions, not to have power, and they share it for the good of all humankind. When I sit and listen to the many women from around the world who have studied and researched the pressing issues affecting women, I can only be humbled and grateful for the opportunity. The warmth and sincerity is so evident; we all work for a common purpose.

Looking back at 2012, I have to wonder what our common purpose as Malaysians is. This year, to me, is a landmark year in incivility, in the type of language and behaviour that could never be associated with good manners and respect. What can we make of people who, in the spirit of misplaced patriotism apparently, thought it appropriate to shake their butts in front of a woman's house?* In the annals of our history, this will not go down as a proud moment. Nor can it be said about the targeting of the individuals, groups of people of different sexual orientation and the hounding of some organisations and online media. I would love to see our leaders go to some international meeting and proudly list these as our achievements this year.

Perhaps in 2013 we have to wait until the elections are over before we return to normal behaviour. Perhaps after that we can carry on with life without finding the need to constantly berate the ones who are most powerless, voiceless and vulnerable. Perhaps we can go beyond a special regulation in Parliament that disallows sexist speech and actually implement a greater respect for women everywhere. Maybe we can stop arguing about why crime seems to have escalated and actually do better policing so that we feel safer. Perhaps, just perhaps, we'll actually restore trust and confidence among the public by actually persecuting someone for major corruption, not just the small fry. Perhaps we can stop displaying our utter lack of confidence in ourselves, especially in matters of faith. Maybe we'll finally have leaders who have the spine to actually tell us what is good public behaviour and what is not. And maybe, just maybe, we'll leave people's private lives alone.

Sadly I don't have the confidence that things will change much after the elections, no matter what the outcome. Whoever loses is going to make everyone's lives miserable by constantly harping on about every little thing they can, including personal stuff, real or otherwise. I don't have the confidence that anyone will behave in mature and magnanimous ways at all. That's partly because of the numerous instances of childish and arrogant behaviour we've seen all year. Will anyone wise up that the public is sick of this? I doubt it.

So what can we ordinary Malaysians do but decide for ourselves what sort of future we want for our country, one that can once again stand proudly in the world, and act on it, not just complain.

Meanwhile I wish everyone a relaxing holiday season, a very Merry Christmas and a new year that restores our faith in this land we all call home. Happy New Year!

*20 December 2012*

*A group of Army veterans performed 'butt exercises' in front of the home of Bersih co-chairman Datuk S. Ambiga in May 2012.

# No Slogans but Action

Sometimes I am prone to wonder what politics, and politicians, are for. Are they there to make life better for us by leading us, or are they there for some other reason which has very little to do with us?

I ask this because despite the ever-shifting election date, there is no doubt that election campaigning has begun. Every day we get told by one side that voting for the other side is a very bad idea. If we vote for one side, we are told, our lives will become even more miserable although it is neither clear how, nor why it would be even more than it is today. The other side, on the other hand, then tells us that voting for the incumbent means more of the same misery.

What is beginning to be obvious to me is that if we vote for either side, we'll wind up miserable. That's hardly what I would call a choice.

The default setting for all our politicians, regardless of who they are, seems to be to automatically disagree with whatever the other side does. Indeed one of our esteemed Ministers was quoted to have said that it is the duty of those on his side of the bench to oppose whatever those on the other side says. That, to me, sounds as if he is also saying 'leave your conscience and your brain to one side and just do what you're supposed to do'.

Which really makes me wonder where that leaves the rest of us. We are wooed like reluctant lovers every five years with every conceivable goodie thrown at us by the incumbent. The other side, not quite having the wherewithal, tries to persuade us that more of the same is not really what we want. They may be right but on the other hand they are not able to tell us what it is that we need either.

There are plenty of issues that I don't trust either side on. For a start, I don't believe that either side is good for women, both being equally conservative. Neither side, for instance, has promised to put more women in ministerial positions. In fact, neither has even mentioned that they would put more women candidates up for election, obviously thinking that this would mean fewer places for male ones. Even if they did have women ministers, what's the bet that they would still hold the 'soft' and 'feminine' ministries, like the Ministry for Women, Family and Community Development or the Ministry of Tourism instead of the more prestigious ones like Finance, Education or Trade and Industry?

Both sides seem to campaign on the premise that voting for the other side means a dubious future. But what I would really like to know is how voting for any side would lead to a bright future. In fact I'd like them to sketch out that bright future for us all, one where we would really be united, working towards some common goals. I'd like to be able to have some hope instead of all the doom and gloom that voting for the 'wrong' side will inevitably bring us. Right now voting for anyone makes me feel like I'm caught between the proverbial devil and the deep blue sea.

It would be great if some of our political leaders would say 'if I were elected, I would bring us all together because we have no time to be disunited'. And really mean it, with real action instead of hiding behind sloganeering.

But why do we even leave our future in the hands of politicians? A recent survey by a public relations company found that most people have very little trust in their politicians, corporations and media. Yet we are still stuck in a system where the running of our country is still entrusted to the very people we mistrust. Every day I find this making less and less sense. There are non-politicians who have much more common sense than the average YB. And really, do we need any special skill beyond common sense to run this country?

I guess what I wish is for normality to return rather than this hate-filled divisive climate that we have to endure these days. If Mitt Romney's campaign sounds like a war on women and anyone who isn't white and rich, our election campaigns sound like a war on everybody, even though it is the same 'everybody' who has to vote our government in. If that makes sense, I don't get it.

Maybe what we should do is instead of the political parties putting up candidates, we the people should just name whom we want and vote them in, regardless of affiliation. I bet we'd really get a good team there.

*25 October 2012*

## Electoral Shopping List

One morning, my breakfast was marred by someone with a loudhailer announcing a political ceramah in my neighbourhood. Then I found an infestation of political party flags and banners by the roadside near my house. For a moment I thought I must have missed the news: had Parliament been dissolved already?

In a few days the flags and banners disappeared. Apparently they were put up by one party to coincide with the *ceramah* by another party. How this is meant to influence votes is unclear to me.

Despite so-called rules, it is clear to anyone with a brain that there are lots of people revving up to have an election. In fact some of them have been campaigning already for about two years. Yet nobody has officially announced the general election. Indeed, an official announcement now seems redundant.

So let's just say the general elections are on but only the actual polling day is unknown, a fact that is the source of quite a bit of irritation since nobody can make plans for anything. Everyone is adopting a wait-and-see attitude because they don't know what will happen.

Recently, Prime Minister Julia Gillard of Australia announced their next general election date a full nine months ahead of time. Her reason was that it 'enables individuals, investors and consumers to plan their year. It gives shape and order to their year.' No doubt our year has been bent out of shape because of the constant speculation and maybe it does make sense to have a designated date for the elections like the Americans. Then nobody can pretend that they are not campaigning when in fact they are.

Having said that, obviously the elections are near and what used to be a fairly short silly season has now become an extended one. Some might even say it's overstayed its welcome. Having put up with all manner of ridiculous political one-upmanship for the past year or so, now we have to tolerate even more.

From now on there will only be room for partisanship, not objectivity. There may be many who made up their minds a long time ago but for some of us, it ain't much of a choice. The total bleaghness of one side is only matched by the yuckiness of the other. Perhaps that's why I'm one of the few people who has not received any SMS greetings, invitations to gatherings or boxes of oranges by my local friendly potential candidates. They all know doing any of these things is likely to raise their irritability factor with me.

If any potential government is at all interested in what this one person thinks, I will outline a few things I would tick against their box if I were comparing my choices. You can call it my comparative shopping list.

Firstly I am looking for leadership: a statesman or woman who is ready to make a stand about what's right and what's wrong, someone who's not scared of every shadow in case shadows vote. I'd like someone who knows how to draw the line between good behaviour and bad, and doesn't throw up their hands to disclaim responsibility when other parties behave badly obviously on their behalf. I cannot possibly teach my children good manners and ethics if there are public bad examples like these.

Secondly, I am looking for bridge-builders and peacemakers, the sorts of people who know how to dial down the temperature, not raise it up for political expediency. I'd like to see someone who reaches out and builds bridges with sincerity, and doesn't feel the need to bring along lots of media when he or she does it.

Thirdly, I really want a politician to say out loud that he or she believes that men and women are equal. Really, is it that difficult?

Fourthly, I'd like to hear someone say that we are part of the community of nations of the world and we will stop thinking we are different and better in everything. There are global standards that we should adhere to, and some so-called 'poorer' countries are doing better than us in some areas. Otherwise no need for participation at international forums or even study tours because what would be the point?

Fifthly, when someone says they want us to be progressive, they really mean it in every way. Not just in terms of technology and hardware but also in attitudes towards education, towards women and young people, towards those in need.

And sixthly, I'd like 'moderate' to mean in terms of spending, in terms of politicking, in terms of word and deed. And that moderation is not just for foreign consumption but also for us at home.

Surely that's a shopping list that isn't too difficult to fulfil?

*28 February 2015*

# Women Still Running Behind in the Elections

Once again we are in election mode and once again candidate lists are checked to see who might be running our country next. Some old faces are gone, some are still there but there are also many new ones. Perhaps also there is more drama this time, what with people who were expected to stand missing, standing as independents and other bizarre cases. Elections are obviously when you get to know the true nature of people.

As always, I scrutinised the lists to see how many women are standing this time. The Election Commission says that there has been a 40% increase in the number of women candidates this time. It looked like women are finally being given the chance they deserve to represent half the population.

But upon closer inspection, the numbers are not as pleasing as they may seem. Yes, the overall numbers of women candidates have increased. But as a percentage of the total number of candidates, they are still make up only about 10% of those in the running.

This is extremely disappointing. In the last Parliament, women made up only 10% of the total number of MPs while in the state assemblies, women were a dismal 8%. This is far below the 30% allocation for women designated in the Convention for the Elimination of Discrimination Against Women (CEDAW) which Malaysia has signed and promised to implement. To ensure that we get the 30% of political decisionmakers, it is obvious that we need far more than 30% of nominated candidates to be women. To only have 10% female candidates will mean that even if all of them win, which they won't, we will never meet the target.

It is even more disappointing when there was so much talk about the need to increase the numbers of women in the polls in the days leading up to Nomination Day. Is there a lack of sincerity by the political parties in fulfilling these commitments?

Some have commented on the difficulties in getting women to stand for elections at all. Let us unpack that. In the first place Malaysian politics is a field so tainted by scandalous and boorish behaviour that few women with any self-respect will want to join in. If they did they would have to share space with male politicians who are totally unashamed of their sexist attitudes towards women, and who rarely get reprimanded for them. Indeed, one particularly reprehensible specimen, who regularly tops the list of outrageous male behaviour, is once again defending his seat.

Secondly, women have so much more to consider if they want to stand. Supportive husbands and families are a necessity. There is no way a married woman can enter politics if hubby is sulking at home. Ensuring that the children are cared for while they go campaigning, something men don't have to consider, is another. Furthermore, campaigning is one thing, what if they win? This would necessitate another round of family negotiations and arrangements.

Having said that, since we undoubtedly do need women in Parliament, there is a need to provide some training for aspiring women legislators. It is no use trying to look for women candidates just when elections are pending. If political parties are serious about fielding women, they should start talent-spotting and training women way ahead, perhaps as soon as one election is over. The training would help women to understand what they are up against in the world of legislating and allow them to work through the issues they would face.

One issue would certainly be the condescension of the media towards women politicians, where looks and their personal lives are deemed more important than what they have to say about issues. It is unbelievable that in this day and age, the best that the media can report on women candidates is on their ideas on grooming.

Finally, there are many people who believe that quotas for women are unnecessary and somehow demean women. They say that MPs and ADUNs should be chosen for their capabilities, rather than their sex. It's interesting that it's only when we talk about women in politics (or business) that the question of capability comes up. But 90% of our legislators thus far have been men. Can we in all honesty say that they were all chosen because of exemplary capabilities?

*25 April 2015*

## Still a Man's World, Politically

The election season is upon us in full force and since the day Parliament was dissolved, nomination lists have been scrutinised and re-scrutinised with several dramatic drop-outs and resurrections. It's a soap opera almost worth prolonging.

But nomination day finally arrived and microscopes are out, poring over each and every candidate to see who's who. So far, the fact most remarked on seems to be the numbers of sons, daughters, sons- and daughters-in-law, nephews and brothers (but not sisters) that have been fielded. Which rather makes you wonder if we are becoming like some countries where electoral seats are passed down within families.

My interest, of course, is in how many women candidates have been fielded this time. A rough count has yielded me at least 85 names that I recognise as female (the difficulty is that there are some names whose gender is difficult to ascertain) which is an impressive number. Most of them are in state seats and my impression is that the Opposition has fielded more women candidates than the Barisan. Which is rather interesting, given that at least one of the Opposition parties has always seemed rather women-unfriendly.

I would certainly like to know why political parties have fielded more women this time. Did they heed the call of various women's NGOs and the Women's Ministry to have more female candidates? If so, their response is far from universal, since Perlis has fielded no women candidates at all. To add insult to injury, they fielded one woman candidate in a Parliamentary seat only to take it away from her after a few hours. Another woman incumbent lost her seat to her own brother, which leads you to wonder why they couldn't have found him another seat instead of taking hers away?

Three women won their seats uncontested. At least one of them won due to the incompetency of her potential rival, but it would have been good to know what the mettle of the other women actually is, gauged through an actual election battle. Several women candidates are pitted against other women candidates, leading us to wonder if the sex of the candidate is a factor at all. In any case, we should celebrate since, win or lose, we will have a woman representative in.

Some people have asked why it is necessary to be concerned about the numbers of women elected representatives. Why, they ask, can't we just choose people based on ability rather than sex?

The thing is, politics, by and large, is a man's game. It is stacked against women in every way, from the finances needed to run for office, to the long hours, to the types of issues that are promoted. When women come in, they are pressured not to push for any women's issues because these are seen as 'discriminatory' against men. They are supposed to be 'gender-neutral' instead.

But gender-neutrality is not the same as gender equality when the playing field between men and women is not level. When the head of the state-level Wanita branch can be denied a seat because someone's brother wants it, it makes for a strong argument to have seats reserved for women. Otherwise everybody's brother, son, son-in-law or nephew will elbow out every woman candidate available, especially when the one who has the final say is a man.

Still, having more women representatives does not necessarily mean better representation. But the higher numbers are more likely to yield more quality representatives than low numbers of women. Besides, women are less likely to make quips about leaks and tunnels*, already a bonus in itself.

We are supposed to be aiming for 30% female representation in elected bodies. That's below the actual proportion of women in the population. Yet still, there are people who think this is too much. Worse still, there are women who are in the position to make this happen who think that we should go slowly on this. As if waiting 50 years isn't slow enough.

There are going to be women representatives who will make blunders because of lack of experience. They will be judged far more harshly than male representatives of similar ilk. It will be seen as a far greater weakness than male incompetence. Sexism prevails unless the women themselves want to change it and will unite, regardless of party affiliation. For that too, they need the numbers in order to be strong. If more women win seats this time, they will gain the confidence to stand up for their rights, or at least for greater respect in the House.

In the meantime, we need to decide who to vote for and get out there and vote. No excuses this time. It's too important.

*27 February 2008*

* A male MP stated in Parliament in 2007 that a female MP 'leaks every month' while the male UMNO assembly speaker at the UMNO General Assembly in Kuala Lumpur said in Malay, referring to air stewardesses with short skirts, 'For some you can even see their tunnel'.

# A Very Malaysian Result

For the last year, it was almost imaginable that we would get to this day, after the General Elections. Everything was put into suspended animation, first because we did not know when the elections would be, then because we did not know what would happen afterwards.

Now we know, and in many ways it was a very Malaysian result. We gave every party just enough; not enough to make anybody ecstatic but enough that they can console themselves that they did partly well. It may not be good enough for the people who want all or nothing but the one thing about democracy is its unpredictability. As Plato said, 'Democracy ... is a charming form of government, full of variety and disorder; and dispensing a sort of equality to equals and unequals alike.'

These elections Malaysians have turned out in record numbers, which speaks well for our growing awareness of the importance of voting. Yet we have kept our cards close to our hearts. I went to several *ceramah*s from both sides in the run-up to polling day and it was difficult to tell who would come out on top. If you stay just within those you agree with, then it is possible to get a distorted view of things. But if you cross over to the other side, you get an idea that nothing is certain. Unlike the cheerleaders, the most circumspect people were also the most cautious and refused to predict a definite outcome.

Perhaps there were a few heightened characteristics of the

election campaign this time. First is the incredible amount of advertising being thrown at voters from every possible direction. You can't drive anywhere without seeing banners and posters, some of which should have been taken down by JPJ for obstructing the view of drivers. Social media talks about nothing else and even the most innocuous update gets connected to politics. You can't even play games online without having to first endure a political video.

To be sure, the campaign advertising war was hugely one-sided to the point of overkill. Besides banners, posters, billboards and T-shirts, there was the free merchandise. I once counted 12 different types of merchandise in one 'markas'. I'm still wondering how wing-mirror covers win elections. The money could have been better used to provide information on what candidates stood for and where you could meet them.

In the last days of campaigning, three human traits became obvious: fear, paranoia and mistrust. All sides used fear to create paranoia and mistrust and unfortunately many allowed themselves to be used by politicians in that way. It made some Malaysians turn against other Malaysians and tolerance, understanding and respect went out of the window. This is not the future that we expected where all humans would enjoy equal rights. Instead, we fell to making distinctions between one human and another, based on suspicion and conjecture. We should really reflect on how easily this ugly side of us came out when provoked.

No doubt we can blame various parties for creating an atmosphere in which this was possible. But we fell for it. In the name of democracy, we became undemocratic.

But this is the day after and we have to move on. Again, do

we rely on our leaders of whatever stripe to lead us in moving on or do we do it ourselves? As the ever-cynical writer Gore Vidal said, 'Democracy is supposed to give you the feeling of choice, like Painkiller X and Painkiller Y. But they're both just aspirin.'

My feeling is that we will learn from this and we will focus on the next elections where we will insist that all sides have to earn our trust and therefore our votes. I don't think we will succumb to manipulation any more. I also think that the most crucial reform needed is in the media that truly needs to redeem itself from its outrageous behaviour during the campaign, dispensing with any semblance of objectivity or balance. We need to demand from the media an accounting of how much it thinks it contributes to national unity and healing. The people voted out the worst proponents of disunity and the media should take heed of that.

Meanwhile, we have to watch as a new government takes shape. I would really advise the PM to stop thinking of Cabinet posts as a form of reward but rather as assigning tasks of huge responsibility. For that he should not choose the same old faces. To really show he is sincere about change, his criteria for his ministers should be talent, youth and gender, three things that were wholly absent before. Only then will we believe this is a fresh new beginning.

*9 May 2013*

# Have Some of Us Lost the Plot?

Although this is my first column for 2014, I'm actually writing it still in 2013. So let's call this a transitional column with a review of the past year and maybe some hopes for the coming one.

Personally, 2013 was not a bad year for me. I made two resolutions at the beginning of it which I have mostly kept. One was to brush up my French, so I have been going fairly regularly to classes all year. The other was to keep a diary, and I'm happy to say that I've written something every day for at least 340 days in 2013.

But I can't say the same for our beloved country. 2013 was a year in which we became more fractious, more disunited, more angry. Some people, to my mind, have completely lost the plot. It was a year where a regular occurrence, general elections, became the excuse for so much rancour on all sides, and afterwards, very little self-reflection. We now have a government in power which is disliked but yet unable to understand why that is so. And is responding by thinking that all people want is more religion and to be bought.

Even then it is failing miserably. Throwing monetary goodies at people, as any fool should know, is a short-term measure. People want to feel good all the time, not just for a day or two. There is a simple premise behind election promises and pledges: they need to be kept. Either that or rely on people's short term memory – which isn't reliable by any measure.

It's astounding to me that simple logic doesn't apply to the way our politicians think. If you want people to like you, just be nice to them. And being nice doesn't include finding bogeymen under every rock and being nasty to them. We don't want our lives enhanced through the misery of others; we'd like everyone to be happy, thank you.

It's plain to any intelligent Malaysian (and dear Government, there are more of us than you think) that all this going after small groups of defenceless people is just a distraction. If 1500 people are a danger to us all just because they have slightly different beliefs, then we are bestowing on them more power than they have. Similarly with all the other dangers and insults we keep dreaming up. All it shows is that we are a weak people and 'they' are incredibly powerful.

We are now being led by people who are ignorant, unschooled and yet proud to be so. We have celebrated the Gregorian New Year forever, how did it suddenly become a Jewish celebration*? We have wished our fellow Malaysians the best during all our festivities, how did it suddenly become a threat to our faith? Or is our faith so fragile that it can hardly withstand anything? The other day I had to worry about what paper I wrapped a gift in, in case the recipient got offended. This is how ludicrous it has become.

But what is truly ludicrous is the silence from the top. What sort of leadership do we have which only mouths platitudes about moderation and unity, yet has absolutely nothing to say about the type of extreme pronouncements made not only by so-called NGOs but also by some parts of government? Are they oblivious or scared? And if they are scared, why?

Once upon a time we used to say 'Malaysia Boleh', that Malaysians were capable of achieving anything. Today we might as well say 'Malaysia Tak Boleh' because every day there are more and more things that we are told we cannot do. We are told we cannot be nice to each other because it might endanger the faith of some of us. We are told that we cannot talk frankly because some people, obviously with weaker constitutions than the rest of us, might get offended. We cannot do anything without treading on eggshells because some people have paper-thin skins.

So basically the Malaysians we are most supposed to be proud of are those with weak faith, who need constant government help and  have such an inferiority complex that anything and everything that anyone else does better is offensive to them. These are the people who think that the fastest way to heaven is to oppress other people. Lovely!

And our leader would rather spend time defending family foibles than to speak up for the most vulnerable and defenceless in society. How embarrassing is that?

So my wish for 2014 is that more Malaysians will wake up and realise the danger our country is in. That to survive in the world today is by being strong. And strength comes from being educated and in tune with the realities of the world, not living in some fantasy land filled with bigots.

*11 January 2014*

---

* Datuk Mustapha Idrus, president of the Malaysia International Institute of Islamic Cooperation (Ikiam), was reported to have said that New Years' celebrations reflected Jewish culture.

## Being Led Astray

I've said this before but sometimes I feel that our leaders live in a parallel universe from us, the citizens. This past week is no exception.

Our esteemed leader goes to New York and talks up the country he rules in a way which we don't recognise. It's all hunky-dory here, he said, we are doing fine. This, despite the choking haze, the drastic drop in the ringgit, the mounting divisiveness among people caused by politics, the curbing of any media or people who are trying to get accurate information to people about what's going on, the hounding of anyone who has different ideas, opinions, lifestyles and faiths, court judgements that rule that the majority of the population have no rights under our Constitution, not to mention an ongoing financial scandal which has yet to be explained by anyone. We have a leader who, embarrassingly, is being investigated by no less than the FBI and yet he swans into New York as if everything is OK. Now that's what I call seeing the world through rose-tinted glasses.

To add to that, we hear from New York that child marriage is no problem at all in Malaysia (despite the Government's own statistics) and it only happens in cases 'such as legalising out of wedlock pregnancies and preventing social misconduct such as free sex, drug abuse and gangsterism, and runaway incidents'. What evidence is there that child marriage prevents 'social misconduct' especially drug abuse and gangsterism? If you marry a child off to a drug user, chances are she'll turn into one too. I hope the jaws of the other participants at that seminar dropped upon hearing this. There was even a factual mistake in the speech. No, it is not true that 70% of our girls are enrolled in universities but, yes, it is true that the enrolment in our universities is 70% girls. See the difference?

It is one thing to want to say good things about our country when abroad, but at the same time, why neglect or distort the facts? A quick check on Google will reveal that things are not as rosy as all that. Then you wind up looking silly, or as if you don't know much about your own country.

Which may be completely true, as a matter of fact. You know only the version of the country that suits you.

Well let me tell you about the real version of this country. People are choking under so many things these days. It's not just the haze, which God knows is a truly disgusting man-made phenomenon that is probably going to affect our health for generations. Already I know of one person who has died because of an asthma attack likely made worse because of the haze. Who knows how many others there are?

The haze is simply the 'icing' on an already stressed-out people, stressed out by rising costs of living, by instability, by uncertainty. We have a national education system which produces students fit for not much, which is being abandoned in droves by parents who are scrimping to send their kids elsewhere. Yet our politicians keep repeating that old mantra that Chinese schools need to be eliminated for unity's sake. Why just pick on them? Why not religious schools, private schools, international schools and home-schoolers as well? Don't they also contribute to the fragmentation of our young people, along racial, religious and class lines? What do these politicians have to say about the thousands of non-Chinese kids in Chinese schools? Isn't China our big buddy now and we need to learn how to speak to them?

Our other big buddy is of course the US but are we learning to speak to them too? If our children's ability to speak English has become so poor, how do we expect them to work out how to deal with the onslaught of US-made goods that now have even more access to our markets than before, with the TPPA? How are they supposed to read the labels and instructions? Are we planning to translate all those labels and manuals? But how is anyone even going to afford to buy any of those goods with the ringgit the way it is? Oh I forget, someone said our pathetic ringgit is good for tourists.

The real version of Malaysia is much tougher and grittier than our delusional leaders make it out to be. But what do they care? Our money is being thrown down the drain on all sorts of ridiculous 'deals' from doubtful loans and property acquisitions to renting pandas at astronomical costs. What has speaking at the UN, ironically at a summit to end poverty, got to do with anything that a regular Malaysian citizen experiences here?

*October 2015*

# True Leaders

I am often asked if there will ever be a woman prime minister in this country. My answer to that is always no. The current system is stacked against women, regardless of whichever party they might be. It is difficult for women to become prime minister on their own merit.

But it is interesting to me that people, many of them men, should keep asking me this. I think it is because people are tired of the lack of talented leaders in this country that they want a different type altogether. And it might as well be a woman.

Our country is facing a leadership crisis. We only have nominal leaders, not real ones. We have people who are put in positions of leadership whether they have the talent for it or not. And unfortunately most of the time they are decidedly talentless.

For instance, a true leader would have some vision of where they want to take the country to. But more importantly they would be able to articulate that vision over and over again so that people know that he (or she) is consistent and committed to it. Instead, not only do we not know what the vision of our leaders is but they remain completely inconsistent, chopping and changing as they please. This confuses people, and yet they have the gall to blame others for that confusion.

A real leader steps up to the plate when things go wrong. They have personal values and principles which drive them and they are not afraid to stand up for them. Thus if anyone says or does something which they find abhorrent, they will speak out, even when the offender might be someone on their side. To them, when something is wrong, it is wrong, regardless of who does it. It is not wrong only when people they don't like do it, and right when people they like do it.

Sadly, what we often see are leaders without principles, ready to follow wherever the loudest voices are. They actually believe that loud is might and soft is meek, and therefore are ready to sacrifice the majority for the interests of a few. Over time their consciences become hardened until they sleep soundly at night despite the many wrongs they are committing daily.

A true leader speaks no words but his own, because those are the only ones that are authentic to him. He will not speak the words of others, especially without vetting them first. He has no need for disturbing visuals, as if he was speaking to a class of illiterate schoolchildren who would not understand a single word he said otherwise. He would be wise enough to know that to manipulate people's emotions through images is the lowest trick in the book.

No leader worth his salt believes his own public relations. To bask in false glory, boosted by artificial means, is what fools do. A leader needs to be clear-eyed about his own popularity, and to be humble about it. There is nothing more grotesque than a leader puffed up with pride and hot air.

Such a leader would get away with it if there was nothing to compare him with. Unfortunately, within his neighbourhood he has counterparts far more visionary and certainly far more humble than he. Unfortunately too, we live in an age in which we can follow what other leaders do very closely. And then we find our own wanting.

Leadership by example is not a new concept. But what examples are our leaders setting? When they can be humble, they are instead full of hubris. When they can be kind, they are instead uncaring especially of the poor and marginalised. When they have the opportunity to do the right thing, they don't. When they can be gracious, they are not.

Is it any wonder then that people learn from these examples to be arrogant, uncaring and even corrupt? When we look at the number of incidences of people being simply unkind to each other, sometimes violently, doesn't it make us wonder why it is happening? Could it be that unkindness is all that they see from our leaders and they therefore equate that with power over others? Rather like abused children who become abusers themselves, abused citizens are just as likely to do the same.

It is totally weird logic to say that violence in the form of draconian laws is the only way to ensure stability. This is a bit like saying that if we beat our children every day, they will become obedient. They may indeed cower in submission. But they will grow up twisted and unhappy.

Perhaps it is time we abandoned the colonial system of having our leaders chosen by only a few and chose them directly instead.

*4 December 2014*

# Madiba's Example

Some 16 years ago I had the opportunity to meet Nelson Mandela at a private dinner that I invited myself to. My parents were there as was Graca Machel, soon to be his wife. I don't remember anyone else being there, perhaps our then High Commissioner to South Africa. But it was a dinner I shall never forget.

Madiba (his clan name) was friendly and charming. He did not look like a man who only a few years before had spent 27 years in prison, some of it in solitary confinement. He told stories of his past with no trace of bitterness or rancour, and exhibited a joy in life that was infectious.

After dinner we were standing around when Madiba decided to approach me. He had heard I was working in HIV/AIDS, a cause for which he was a passionate champion, especially since South Africa had the highest percentage of people, 20%, infected with HIV at the time. 'What you're doing,' he said, 'is so important. You must keep at it.'

I'd like to say that we had a long-drawn-out conversation. But the truth is that I was so overwhelmed by being spoken to so personally by Nelson Mandela that I could barely talk. All I could think of was that he knew of my work and was giving me advice and the thought rendered me speechless. I do remember that we did take some photographs but I don't know where they are. But they cannot have been very good. Madiba's eyes had suffered a great deal from his years in Robben Prison so he could not tolerate camera flashes. So we took a photograph in very bad light without the flash.

I think the aura and charisma of the great man emanated to all who saw him. He walked through the hotel lobby and everybody stopped to watch him and to say hello. He had such a twinkle in his eyes and a great big smile that there was nobody who could stay sombre in his presence. The next day we waved him off at the airport and it really felt like our lives seemed lessened by his absence.

I had another opportunity to hear him speak at the World AIDS Conference in Bangkok in 2004. Once again he was powerful and persuasive in his message to end the stigma and discrimination against People Living with HIV. But I did not get to meet him. Instead, I was immensely flattered and honoured to share a panel with his wife Graca Machel and to find that she actually remembered me. She is truly a gracious woman who lives up to her name.

Watching Graca Machel's sorrow at Madiba's funeral was truly heartbreaking. You felt his absence in her life but you also felt his absence in the whole world. Leaders such as Mandela are so rare these days that to lose him feels a bit like not having enough oxygen. All around us we see so-called leaders who do not lead, who care nothing about moving our country forward and who cause disunity and instability while at the same time accusing others of the same. We have people in power who have not tasted anything close to the suffering that Mandela did, yet have the gall to compare themselves to him and their party's struggles to his. Our leaders have no charisma and everything they say makes us angry or depressed, never uplifted. Worse, they are bent on blaming others for their failures and being revengeful.

Nelson Mandela suffered immeasurably during his years in prison. Yet he emerged ready to forgive and bring about reconciliation instead of seeking vengeance against those who oppressed him and his people. He set an example not just for his people but also for all of us the world over.

What example, on the other hand, have our so-called leaders set for us? That power is to be used to go after those who are weakest and least able to defend themselves? What bravery! That those who don't agree with them should be shut up? What gallantry! That those who oppose should be punished as much as possible? Such magnanimity!

Suffice to say that none of our leaders should ever be mentioned in the same breath as Nelson Mandela. Because none of them are capable of ever saying this: 'No one is born hating another person because of the colour of his skin, or his background or his religion. People must learn to hate, and if they can learn to hate, they can be taught to love. Because love comes more naturally to the human heart than the opposite.'

Farewell Madiba, rest in peace.

(And to everyone, Merry Christmas and a Happy New Year.)

*21 December 2013*

# A Pillar of Strength

Sometimes people come into your life and you can't foresee what impact they are going to make. Last week many of my colleagues and I mourned the death of Puan Sri Naimah Hasbi after a long illness. In the newspapers, she was recognised only as the wife of the former Minister Tan Sri Sulaiman Daud. In fact she was much much more.

I can't remember when I first met Puan Sri Naimah but in 1993 she welcomed me to a dinner that ended with my being made the Chair of the Malaysian AIDS Foundation. Puan Sri was a founding trustee and remained so until her death last Saturday, 26 March. Many people of her standing sit on Boards and do little but Puan Sri was not one of those. She not only came to every single meeting of the Board and took an interest in everything that was discussed but also attended every event and function we organised during all those years, if she was in town and available. If we asked her to attend something on our behalf, she always graciously obliged. She chaired for a time our Paediatric AIDS Fund committee that provided financial support to children infected with and affected by HIV/AIDS.

It was not just Puan Sri Naimah's commitment that inspired us all. Her attitude towards everything was an example to everyone. She was always cheerful and interested. Never one to have airs, she would come to our events, armed with her ever-present camera and mix around with everyone, including people living with HIV/AIDS, as naturally as if they were her own friends and neighbours. Perhaps she had more empathy than most with those who had problems. Unlike many, she was willing to learn, often coming to seminars to listen and to ask questions. Always she was clearly sincerely sympathetic to people with HIV/AIDS and was never one to make judgments on people.

Helping others came naturally to Puan Sri. If she felt that it would benefit someone to meet and discuss an issue with another party, she would organise it and even host it at home. If she heard that someone had arthritis and felt they would benefit from massage, she would personally take the person to the masseuse. How she fit in all this helpfulness while managing a home and family as well as her commitments to several other organisations is a wonder to us all. But you could always count on her.

We will all remember Puan Sri Naimah for her openness and her courage in the face of her own illness. She never hid the fact that she had cancer. Often she would come to meetings and cheerily announce that she had just come from her chemotherapy treatment. Never once did she display any self-pity. Indeed she remained her perfectly dressed self, determined to not let her illness dictate her life, until almost the end.

A year ago, Tan Sri Sulaiman quietly requested us not to invite his wife to any more meetings because he did not feel she was up to it. She herself did not think so and occasionally an invitation would slip through and she would drive herself to our office, perfectly turned out as always. But it was clear then that her husband was right to worry. Puan Sri was lucky in having a caring husband and family who never left her side throughout her illness. They too are an inspiration to us all for their unending love and dedication.

Many of us working in HIV/AIDS in Malaysia will miss Puan Sri Naimah. She was like a mother to us all, gently pushing us along the difficult roads. She showed us that with care, compassion and courage, we can tackle anything.

May God bless her soul and may she rest in peace. Al-Fatihah.

*6 April 2005*

# The Cost of Telling the Truth

When parents try to teach their young children certain values and behaviours, consistency is the key. When you tell children that lying is wrong, then they must never catch you telling untruths. If you say there's no money to buy some fancy new toy, then you can't come home with a brand new car without them wondering how come you can afford that. Children have natural radar for hypocrisy. It is tuned to catch any inconsistencies, white lies or complete untruths that parents spout because these grate against the natural sense of fairness that kids have. And every time they catch their parents out, a small bit of parental authority erodes.

This anti-hypocrisy radar is only maintained if the child doesn't then learn that to be hypocritical is more rewarding than to be true to one's own conscience. If they find that there is nothing to be gained from telling the truth, and everything to gain from fudging facts, then the child grows up with their moral compass askew. They learn not to take responsibility for their own misdeeds but to blame others for it. Thus you get stories, for example, about kids who blame their maids for not putting their homework in their schoolbags on the day they are meant to pass it.

Unfortunately, there are more and more adults behaving in this way these days. I can only assume that once they did have a conscience, believed in certain things but along the way grew to learn that being true to that conscience is no way to get ahead in life. As children, they might have had a strong sense of justice, of instinctively knowing when something is unfair. But when they become adults, that instinct is put aside because it's not a ticket to advancement. Besides if everyone else is doing it, why be the exception?

To be the exception requires the strength of moral character that is able to withstand the pressures that come from others, whether family, colleagues or bosses. It also requires the courage to take whatever blowback that might come from standing one's ground, some of which undoubtedly will have implications to more than one's self. But for those with such courage, the greatest reward is the ability to sleep at night, knowing their conscience is clear.

These days I find myself wishing I knew more people of such moral fortitude because they do seem thin on the ground. I see people who have no qualms about making themselves popular by preaching the oppression of those who have no voice. I shudder to read of people who blithely believe that the rule of law should only apply to themselves but not to others. If one were ever to accuse them of any crime, they immediately plead that they are innocent, but they accord no such consideration to those they don't like. They say that those of us who open our mouths in protest have no respect for the law, when they themselves barely hesitate to override those very same laws.

The tragic thing is that these types of people think they are leaders, because in the popularity contests they indulge in, they win. Never mind if their means of winning would hardly fit a child's description of fairness, what matters most is that they win. I look at the lineup of the so-called leaders we have and I have to despair. Not a single one of them would be anyone I would look up to. None are names that would come immediately to mind as those who could take us confidently into the future, to take our place among the best in the world. Instead I see people whose minds remain in an ancient age where might is always right, and the majority always wins. And a fat wallet is everything.

Many years ago I was in a country much poorer than ours where I met a young politician who seemed just the type of dynamic leader the country needs. There were rumours that he would stand for election as the mayor of their capital city. But when I asked him, he replied that he was not going to. 'It takes a million US dollars to have a running chance of winning that post', he said. It wasn't that he did not have the money because he came from a wealthy family but he did not feel that was the right thing to do.

Today I saw a quote about how much it takes to stand for party elections in our country. It costs four times more to run for elections in a party of three million members than to stand for mayor of a city of 18 million.

Enough said.

*31 October 2013*

# Lessons from Animals

I've just watched a fascinating lecture on whether animals have morals. In various laboratory experiments, it's been shown that capuchin monkeys and dogs do care about how their friends feel. If they see a friend in pain, they will try and comfort them. If they see that getting a food reward means that their friend will suffer from an electric shock, they will forego food rather than subject their friend to such pain. They will help one another to get the same rewards, although they won't help someone they don't know. And they seem to have an inherent sense of fairness, rejecting attempts to being differently rewarded for the same tasks.

So in many ways they are the same as human beings. What's different of course is that they don't tend to sit around and analyse why all this happens. The other big difference is that they also don't tend to punish those who transgress these rules. So they might protest at unfair treatment or go on a hunger strike in support of a friend, but they don't seek to punish perpetrators of such unfairness.

The experiments also found that capuchin monkeys are quite willing to support other capuchin monkeys that they know and can see but not those they don't know and can't see. Their first priority is their kith and kin and not strangers, especially anonymous ones. This also differentiates them from humans who will extend a hand to total strangers such as we did during the tsunami and Typhoon Haiyan, with no expectation of reward.

These studies show that although sometimes we claim that morality in humans is determined by culture and religion, some things are probably hardwired into us. We all have an innate aversion to harm, an inherent sense of fairness, respect for authority and care for our young. Studies on babies and toddlers have shown that they will cooperate and help others without being asked. This tends to dissipate though as they get older, though it never really disappears since we do see the same traits in adults too. One explanation is that if we stopped cooperating with one another, pretty soon the human race will simply die off because we do need one another to survive.

The lecture also compared not just morality in animals and humans but also immorality, specifically violence against others. I presume violence was chosen because it's a bit difficult to assess lying and cheating in animals since we don't speak their language. And in some things, such as sexual behaviour, we can't really impose our human values onto them.

The best comparisons are with our closest genetic relatives, chimpanzees and bonobos. These two groups of animals may seem similar but behave in very different ways. Chimpanzee society is an extremely violent one. They not only fight each other within their own community but also others in other communities and are prone to physical abuse of the female members of their community and infanticide. The primate expert Jane Goodall studied two communities of chimpanzees in Gombe, Tanzania which engaged in a four-year war which ended with all the males in the smaller community being killed and the females absorbed into the larger community. The war was not limited to skirmishes when the two communities chanced upon one another. The larger one would actually send out raiding parties to seek out and viciously attack members of the smaller one, especially those seen as weak.

Bonobos, on the other hand, are an extremely peaceful society, preferring, literally, to make love and not war. They never attack each other or outsiders and seem to spend most of their time being very affectionate with one another. The explanation for this is that female bonobos, unlike chimpanzee females, bond with one another very tightly and stand in solidarity with one another. As a result they are able to temper the male instinct for violence and this results in an overall peaceful society.

There may well be many traits we might recognise in ourselves in our primate cousins. It's worth noting that the only two species that actually wage war on others are chimpanzees and humans. But there are some differences. For while chimpanzees rely only on their own strength for warfare, humans go on to develop very sophisticated weapons that can kill thousands of strangers thousands of miles away, often without even leaving home.

And if we learn anything from our bonobo cousins, it's that a society that gives their females a big say in how things are run tends to be a more peaceful one. Easy to see which type of society is likely to advance.

Given the recent monkey-like behaviour we are seeing in our country, we should ask ourselves: are we chimpanzees or bonobos?

*14 February 2014*

# Many Things Do Not Make Sense

There are many things that I love about this country that I was born in and have lived in my whole life. But when it starts to give me knots in my stomach and a constant feeling of dread, I can't help but wish it were another type of country, one where everybody feels easy and comfortable living in it.

It would be alright if things that happen actually make sense but every day things make less and less sense. I am starting to dream about living in a different type of country where everyone can go their own way and live in peace without harassment from anyone.

In another type of country, people are not afraid to apologise when they've done something wrong. Indeed, they come out as more honourable people. Instead we have people whose main stock in trade is hubris. It is what makes them unable to lift charges against people who have done no wrong, leaving them forever in suspended animation. Hubris is what makes some people unable to backtrack on a mistake they made, finding ever more convoluted justifications for it. Pure arrogance is what makes them disobey court orders and say they answer to nobody else. Never mind that this is exactly the sort of attitude that leads to the anarchy that they themselves fear.

In another type of country, the police would just follow the law and not think up interpretations that keep them sitting on their hands in the face of injustice. Especially when it involves children and the mothers they should always be with, by any type of law.

If this was another type of country, when people have been slack at their jobs and this led to many fatalities, they would resign. We now know that had some people paid better attention and taken some quick action, the fate of MH370 might not be still a mystery today, more than 100 days after it disappeared. In another country, the highest officials in charge of our skies would have stepped down from their jobs because that is the honourable thing to do. But who cares about honour or respect in this country?

If we were another type of country, we would stop declaring war on our own people. The so-called war on drugs has stopped neither drug trafficking nor drug addiction. Now we are going to have a war on the homeless. Without understanding the reasons why people are living on the streets, a war on them would be akin to waging a war on refugees and blaming host countries for being too generous while doing nothing about the violence in their home countries that drove them to leave in the first place. But it is so much easier to declare war than to wage peace. Ask George Bush.

If we were a rational compassionate country, we would be declaring a war on the increasing violence against women and children and stop the abuses, gang rapes, kidnappings and murders. How do our officials tasked with protecting women and children justify their existence otherwise?

If we were a sensible country, we would stop lauding the mean and the vile as heroes. We would stop fearing the consequences of showing compassion and fairness towards those suffering injustice. We would just be plain decent folk doing the right thing by people.

If we were a normal country, we would never be proud of being unable to control ourselves and possibly inflicting violence on others. We would never insist on having laws to keep ourselves under control, even while we claim to be pious. In fact normal people are usually ashamed to describe themselves as having potential for violence. But we are not living in a normal country anymore.

If this was another country, the very idea of chopping off anyone's hands for stealing or stoning people for adultery would be too repulsive to even discuss. But today these punishments are what people seriously think will solve all our problems. The bankruptcy of ideas is there for all to see.

If this were a place where things made sense, a woman could never be divorced years after her husband died. Or get her wedding interrupted by officials from another religion. Or have her burial delayed because of a long-forgotten alleged conversion. Or have her underaged children taken away from her by a husband who converted to another religion. Isn't it funny how these things always seem to happen to women?

Yet we were once a civil and progressive country. Where people respected one another and got on fine. Once we eschewed violence of any kind, and certainly not against one another. Today we even go to foreign countries and blow ourselves up.

We are no longer the country we once were. The question is, why?

*19 June 2014*

## Stop Embarrassing the Public

I was observing recently how different people had different definitions of shame. Most define it as a sense of embarrassment when something they cannot control happens. For instance, one person said it was what he felt every time he saw a foreign tourist go into a public toilet. Another said it's when she can't repeat what she just said in front of her kids.

I was curious about this because of the way the word 'shame' kept coming up in relation to recent events. There were some people who felt shame that Malaysians had taken to the streets in protest because they felt that this was 'uncivilised' behaviour. Then there were others who saw shame in the opposite perspective: they felt embarrassed that their fellow citizens were treated so badly by the authorities. Surely, they said, we have become civilised enough to tolerate dissent without having to react to it with violence. Thus 'shame' and 'civilised' behaviour appeared on both sides of the fence.

Then there were those who felt embarrassed and ashamed that a minister could expose himself as an inarticulate buffoon on international TV. The minister in question however felt no shame at all, even repeating the whole sorry spectacle on his own TV channels with great pride. Herein lies the puzzle: how is it that poor performance can invoke pride rather than shame? Is that symptomatic of something else these days?

In the old days (which don't seem too long ago), people did

not talk about parts of the body or bodily functions in public especially at inappropriate moments. But these days we get parliamentarians and other public officials making crude remarks, almost always about women's anatomy and bodily functions, without even so much as turning the slightest shade of red. And what do their audiences do when they hear this? They giggle and laugh. Perhaps, secretly, the mostly female audience felt shame and embarrassment but, because they are dependent on male authority figures for their positions, they say nothing and played along instead. And in so doing they betrayed their own sex once again. How little we value our dignity.

These are the times when I feel so old-fashioned. Which people may find ironic considering that I am accused of being shameless a lot for wanting to talk about sex education for young people and about how to make sex safe. But the one thing one never does when educating others about sex is to make it crude, because that's what turns people off. Appropriate terminology and approach is key.

But outside of the educational context, when the intention is to humiliate, referring to the anatomy is crude and unnecessary. People should be embarrassed not only to have to listen to it but also to even mention it. Thus I wonder at what point will we decide that our tolerance for such crudeness has finally reached its limit. When are we truly going to censure public figures who talk trash regardless of their station in life? When are we going to shame them into stopping?

Instead we see endless shows of shamelessness. There are public figures who build humongous mansions with unexplained funds and then try to look charitable by inviting orphans to a one-night stay. I blush at the thought of it, how come they don't?

Others, obviously endowed by the thickest of skins, buy support by giving out honorifics even to those who patently do not deserve them or even have criminal records. Not an ounce of shame whatsoever. Everyone else laughs at them but they actually think they are being exemplary human beings. No shame in the least about redefining humanity as being corrupt. Incredible!

Maybe I should develop a thicker hide. But the thing is I have a young daughter who reads the newspapers and I wind-up red-faced when she asks me how come these people she reads about do and say things which I have always taught her not to. Even though not everything gets into the newspapers (perhaps their limits for shame are lower than those of the people they cover?), my daughter sometimes hears my friends and me talking about the latest public embarrassment. How do I explain these to her?

We need to restore a sense of public shame. To do that, we need to define it and we need leaders who live and behave in exemplary ways. We need leaders who have a sense of diffidence and restrain, who understand that they can't say one thing and do another. Who do not treat the public as if they are fools who will take anything they dish out. That time is no longer far off because we, the public, are beginning to feel we don't want to be embarrassed anymore.

*22 November 2007*

# Oh, the Shame of it All

I wondered this week on the meaning of 'shame'. A statement by an Immigration official, who said that Fatine, a transsexual facing deportation from the UK, had brought 'shame' to Malaysia, prompted my mind to ponder on this word.

By definition, shame is 'a painful emotion caused by a strong sense of guilt, embarrassment, unworthiness or disgrace.' In this case, it seems an overwhelming emotion in response to what is basically someone else's misfortune. After all, nobody knew this poor person until this happened. To then feel shame seems a bit of an overreaction.

This is even more puzzling when shame is never the response expressed over other misdeeds done by Malaysians both at home or abroad. Our citizens have been known to violate immigration laws overseas a great deal. In fact overstaying their visas is almost a Malaysian disease since it is estimated that there are some 30,000 Malaysian over-stayers in the UK. When the UK threatened to stop visa-free entries for Malaysians there recently because of these over-stayers, our authorities organised workshops to help those lawbreakers to come home, assuring them that they would not be arrested and put in prison. How very sweet!

How come we didn't condemn all those people for bringing shame to the country then? Why single out poor Fatine?

Indeed, how come we have never expressed shame at our people who happily break laws in other countries by smuggling drugs and people, cheating, stealing, even murdering? How come Immigration or any other officials don't hold their heads in embarrassment that our people have the temerity to break laws in foreign lands?

How is it that we feel no sense of disgrace when people overseas think we're barbaric for wanting to whip a mother of two for possibly doing herself, and nobody else, personal damage by having an alcoholic drink?

I must say that there have been moments when I have felt great shame at the antics of Malaysians abroad. I feel it at conferences where our officials are obviously missing, only to show up later laden down with bags of shopping. Or when people have taken a lot of trouble to arrange a last-minute visit to a project, and then they don't show up because 'traffic jam lah'.

I felt it when at the conclusion of a short course, which was very expensive and paid for by sponsors, one semi-government participant got an award for 'biggest contribution to tourism', a caustic reference to his frequent absence from class.

I have this tendency to cringe when, at conferences overseas, some of our delegates have nothing to say whatsoever, mostly because they don't know the subject but it was their 'turn' to go. I remember once that the NGO delegation basically wrote the Government statement by default, simply because we knew the subject well and were willing to sit down and work on it.

My face has turned red when I have had to sit through press conferences where Government officials have patently stated untrue things because they sounded good and expounded theories for which there was no empirical basis. There are few things more frustrating than having to squirm through those situations where you are unable to say anything without showing the officials concerned up and, yes, shaming them.

Yet it is people like NGOs who know their stuff who get told off for being disloyal, unpatriotic and supposedly out to embarrass the government. Heck, you may disagree with what we say but at least try and argue as articulately as we do. Then we can hold our heads up and say that our Government officials may get things the wrong way round but boy, they can make a convincing argument for it.

So what is this shame that this official felt? And in fact what has it to do with him at all? Is Immigration in charge of filing charges against our citizens for embarrassing us overseas? Is there anywhere in their regulations that people who 'shame' us overseas will not be allowed to have passports? In that case, there are probably more cases than they can handle.

Our smart official also probably did not think that his words have already travelled the world over and caused many blushes among Malaysians already. What's more, if he carries out his threat, and indeed if anything punitive did happen to Fatine if she returns home, then we would be faced with queries from all over the world with some awkward questions about how we treat the more marginalised sectors of our society.

At a time when we already have more to be ashamed than to be proud of, we really don't need another fiasco, thank you.

*14 December 2009*

## The Anarchy of Bad Manners

I'm usually quite unshockable but occasionally I see something that really knocks my socks off. That was my reaction upon seeing a video recently. It was not pornography or anything mildly like it but it was still horrifying.

In the video, two Caucasian men found that their car had been blocked by a Pasar Ramadan stall. Understandably they asked the stall owner how they might get the car back. Less understandably, the stall owner started screaming at and shoving them. Others joined in and all were shouting and manhandling these two men. Some even yelled at them to 'balik lah...' (go home) although it is unclear where to.

What was shocking to me, besides the fact that this was obviously during Ramadan, when we are meant to exercise restraint, was the sheer over-reaction to something which could have been resolved so easily. Surely it is reasonable to ask someone who is blocking your car what to do about it? Surely the response should have been an apology, followed by an explanation of when the stall would pack up for the night, thereby releasing the car. What was the need for all the shouting, screaming and shoving?

I don't think any civilised person watching this video could have felt anything but embarassed, as I did. What has happened to the *sopan santun* (manners) that we are known for, more so during Ramadan?

I grew up having manners drilled into me and if there's one

thing I am old-fashioned about, that would be it. So I find it hard to understand when people are rude for no apparent reason.

Those who follow me on social media will recall a recent episode when I had to give a little lesson in courtesy to a young man. He has since apologised and I'm sure it wasn't normal behaviour for him. But where would young people learn about manners but from adults?

When we have parliamentarians saying the rudest things to fellow MPs and mostly getting away with it, when we have adult men who think it's funny to go shake their posteriors at a woman's house, when we have people flying off the handle over the simplest things, why would not our young also devalue courtesy and politeness? If you're polite, it is not news and you don't become famous. But if you're crass and crude, you get headlines and everyone remembers your name.

There may be reasons for rage but what I don't get is the infantile way it gets expressed. Name-calling, jeering and shoving is the way of juvenile hooligans, not mature adults. Have we regressed to such a childlike state that those are the only ways we can express rage? What next, mass foot-stomping?

Everything today points towards a society that is encouraged to express itself in mob-like behaviour. One person needs to just say that they are offended by something and, for no rhyme or reason, entire hordes of people decide that they should be offended too. Indeed, they even look at ways to be offended. And when you have leaders who say that the onus is on minorities to behave a certain way so as not to offend the majority, what else could you expect in response?

Are we all supposed to live in such a way that we constantly have to look out for offences imagined in other people's heads? Every time we go out, are we supposed to be always on the lookout for ways to avoid offending total strangers? We might go to a government department where, as taxpayers, we may reasonably expect fast and efficient service. Instead we are treated as if we are offensive creatures because of our choice of clothes.

How does the sight of anyone's legs affect the efficiency of the service? If such a sight is too distracting, even through an opaque desk, then there is something wrong with the person serving the customer, not the customer herself. Why do people whose salaries depend on us paying our taxes get to play both fashion and moral police?

All this could so easily be solved if we had the type of leadership who would come out and say that we should all stop this nonsense about petty things and focus instead on more important issues. For example, how to get our currency to rise again, or how to manage the high cost of living, or how we can work on bringing people together, rather than tearing them apart.

But obviously, with a leadership so silent they might as well not exist, the anarchy of bad manners continues unabated. Is it a symptom of something? Do people get ruder because they feel rudderless? Doesn't anyone want to know?

*2 July 2015*

# That Little Voice in Our Head

I recently attended a conference where the keynote speaker, a renowned academic, talked about science and conscience. One of the slides he showed was a quote from Sophocles, the Greek 'tragedian' or playwright (496–406 BC) which went: 'There is no witness so terrible and no accuser so powerful as conscience which dwells within us.'

In most people the conscience does play a big part in directing the way we behave. It may come from the values our parents or teachers instilled in us or maybe it is something inherent in us, but the conscience is that little nagging voice in us that makes us feel guilty or ashamed when we have done something we shouldn't have. From childhood that voice tells us that taking something that is not ours is wrong, or cheating in exams is unfair or calling people names is hurtful. It's that uncomfortable feeling when we've done one of these things and then didn't own up to or apologise for it.

Everyone has a conscience in one way or another. Some psychologists say that we are born with an innate sense of fairness that either develops or lessens depending on what happens in our lifetimes. In any case, people have enough of a conscience to realise that some actions are regarded as anti-social behaviour and therefore must be hidden from others if done. Consequently nobody openly declares that they are going to steal, cheat or do anything that common sense says we should not, especially if we want to live among other people.

Our conscience is also that nasty feeling in our stomachs when we tell a lie. When we were kids, we knew what would happen if we were ever caught lying to our parents. We might tell them that we had not got our report cards yet but it was difficult to keep a straight face when they kept questioning us about it. Eventually the pressure would become too much to bear and we had to shamefacedly hand over our red-mark-filled card and wait for Dad's fearsome wrath. Those memories of the consequences of lying usually stayed with us until adulthood, training our conscience on the virtues of honesty. As horrible as it may be sometimes, it is usually better to own up when we're at fault.

This assumes that the things we need to own up to are fairly innocuous things, like our age or the fact that we forgot to pay a bill on time. But our conscience can only be burdened with so much; if you do something really terrible, then we need to stop that conscience pricking us or else we cannot sleep at night. Thus we start inventing justifications for the terrible things we did, or start telling ever bigger lies in order to cover up what we did. After a while we start to believe our own lies and even that we never did anything wrong.

I have known some consummate liars and I often wonder how they keep track of every lie they tell. Everything depends on keeping every story unimpeachable, and making sure that nobody is able to compare stories with anyone else. It must be a terrible strain and at some point you're bound to trip up. And that's where things start to unravel.

When they do, there is a mad scramble to keep things together which necessitates more and more lies. That conscience, that nagging voice, that inner compass that tells us where true north is, becomes muffled and ignored altogether. Yet it has a way of peeking out and showing itself in odd ways; the inability to look anyone in the eyes, a voice that isn't convincing, a hand that is shaky. They are signs that can be seen by a shrewd observer though perhaps not by those who prefer not to.

Luckily for societies, not everyone becomes devoid of conscience completely. Otherwise they would become totally lawless and dysfunctional. By and large most people still obey traffic lights because they know it is a good thing to do. And they also get angry at people who don't. They may tolerate the odd person running a red light but not if it becomes an epidemic because obviously it becomes very dangerous for everyone. It is those people who still have their consciences who will save society.

Today, when everything in our society seems to be crumbling, when our leaders have become the ones who run red lights, we have to rely on those traffic cops who still have the conscience to do their jobs correctly, without fear or favour. If we get rid of traffic cops so that we can run red lights with impunity, then we might as well be a society before there were laws regulating our behaviour on the roads.

Imagine if our conscience stopped being our red light.

*13 August 2015*

# A Lack of Consideration

It is almost the end of Ramadan and by right, we would all have learnt patience by now. We try to be patient with the traffic, with slower service, with the general surliness that somehow lack of food brings.

Due to particular circumstances I have been away for most of this Ramadan. So perhaps my patience has not built up as much as others. Which is why mine wore thin when I had to suffer the extremely loud sermon coming from my local mosque early one Sunday morning.

This is not a phenomenon peculiar to Ramadan. In the almost two decades that I have lived in my neighbourhood, my local mosque seems to have acquired a loudspeaker system that progressively enables it to broadcast louder and wider each year. I don't at all mind the azan or the Qur'an-reading that are delivered in very musical styles. Those are soothing and uplifting.

But I do mind the early Sunday sermons. Not just because they are exceptionally loud but because of their tone. For a whole hour, whoever is tasked with delivering the sermon harangues and berates his congregation and, by extension, the entire neighbourhood, for various wrongdoings and sins that apparently we constantly commit.

I've been told off for complaining, and been called arrogant. Apparently when it comes to religion, one must never complain because this would be akin to questioning God. But I can find no reference in the Holy Book that says that sermons must be broadcast so loudly that neighbouring countries are likely to hear them. Indeed in the Great Mosques of Mecca and Medina, you hear nothing outside the mosques apart from the call to prayer.

When mosques are allowed to broadcast as loudly as they want, what exactly do they contribute to the neighbourhood besides disturbing the peace? By haranguing at high pitch in the early hours of the morning, do they portray an Islam that is considerate to the community, many of whom are elderly or non-Muslim? When anyone who complains is accused of arrogance or, if non-Muslim, being anti-Islam, is this accusation not an arrogant message in itself?

To me, this is part of a worrying trend these days where not only do Muslims display a lack of consideration for anyone else, but even for other Muslims. At prayer time, common courtesies within and outside the mosque are no longer commonplace. The mosque is no longer a place for quiet meditation and reflection. Outside cars are nonchalantly triple-parked, with no concern about the traffic jams they cause. Policemen simply turn a blind eye. It seems those who are supposedly going to commune with God can get away with anything.

Once upon a time mosques were community centres catering to the entire community, not just some. They provided shelter to all who came by. In some countries they provide counselling services to anyone who needs it, regardless of religion. Today, they do little to promote peace and harmony in their neighbourhood. Instead they stand as symbols of dominance and power, which nobody can question. Can't we even question why mosques are built with inadequate car parks necessitating the triple parking on the streets outside?

Ramadan is the perfect time for a different type of mosque experience. If fasting is about restraint, why can't the mosque restrain itself from such loud broadcasts of sermons for the entire month? Why should it just be us who have to be extra patient during Ramadan when it is already irritating during other times? Someone said we should just get used to it. That sets a very low bar, akin to asking us to simply get used to bad traffic, pollution and corruption.

Apparently quality of life does not matter, especially when it involves religion. We have to put up with inconvenience on earth because in Heaven we will undoubtedly be rewarded with silent mosques and ample parking.

In other countries, Muslims cannot even build minarets for their mosques. There are moves to ban the azan in those countries. When we get angry about those undoubtedly Islamophobic laws, at the same time it is no excuse for us to overdo things at home, just because we can.

Such annoyances aside, may I take this opportunity to wish everyone a happy and safe Hari Raya Aidil Fitri, *maaf zahir dan batin*. And may the rest of the year be a peaceful and calm one.

Selamat Hari Raya!

*September 2012*

# Time for Restraint, Reflection and Respect

It is the first week of Ramadan and, as always, the body is taking time to adjust. I feel lethargic and sleepy and it takes enormous will to work up the energy to go to work. But bills don't stop needing to be paid, letters answered or columns written during this one month of fasting. I just have to wait a few days before I get used to the daytime deprivation of food and water and will feel normal again.

I like Ramadan because it gives me a sense of a break from the usual routines. Just because there isn't a break in the middle of the day for lunch makes me rework my daily schedule so that I can get home early enough to rest before the breaking of the fast. But I expect there to be days when I work right up till *buka puasa* and won't even notice. Most of all I'm hoping for some benefits from not eating after a year of mostly undisciplined indulgence in all the wrong types of food.

For me, Ramadan is a time of restraint, reflection and respect. By that I mean not just refraining from food and drink but from the worst sides of ourselves. At other times we may be bad-tempered, inconsiderate, gossipy and unthinking but during Ramadan we are supposed to put those sides of us on hold, at least in theory.

I read about how a woman was beaten by her husband because she didn't wake him up early enough for *sahur*. It really makes you wonder why was the spirit of Ramadan, on its very first morning, so lacking that a man could be driven to violence in this way? No doubt there will be some who blame the wife for being 'derelict' in her duty to wake her husband up but I have to ask: could he not have woken himself up, and even if she woke him late, was violence the proper response to this?

Ramadan gives us time to reflect on many things. I like waking up for *sahur* because the early hours of the morning, amidst the cool and the solitude, give me time to think about many things. Sometimes it's just practical things, like making lists of what I have to do for Raya. Other times, it's about what it means to honour the spirit of Ramadan. I try and think of good things I want to be and do and not about things that make me angry or sad. I make a promise to myself to deal with difficult things with greater equanimity.

If people gave themselves time to reflect more during this month, then perhaps they would not do things hastily without thinking of the possible consequences. If you set out to do something obviously insulting, would you not expect some reaction to it? Did you think about how you will deal with this reaction? On the other hand, faced with such blatant attempts at publicity, do we succumb to our basest instincts and provide the reaction that would generate the desired attention? Restraint and reflection should really be practised on all sides, but especially by the ones fasting.

Which leads me to respect, another part of the spirit of Ramadan. Yes, in this country, people need to respect that it is Ramadan and that most people are fasting. But on the other hand, those who are fasting are also obliged to respect others who may not be fasting. We are, compared to many Muslim countries, already one of the most tolerant in that we don't shut down totally just because many of us are fasting. In other countries, they simply turn their daily schedules upside-down. Whatever you do in the daytime, such as eat and work, happens at night instead. In actual fact, precious little work gets done and the whole month becomes festive.

But the practical side of us knows that the world is not going to stop just because some of us are fasting. We still need to work during regular hours because that's when the rest of the world is working. Indeed I'm grateful for this because sleeping all day just makes me grumpy and lethargic.

But fasting doesn't mean we have an excuse to do shoddy work. That means we have no respect for our work and those who employ us. Nor does it give us a licence to demand respect from others. To say that others have to be extra-respectful or sensitive to us because we are fasting is demeaning and disempowering. It is a bit like being disabled and asking for more crutches to shore up our weaknesses.

Ramadan is, after all, the time to show the strength of our faith, our spirit and our discipline.

*20 July 2013*

## Staying Happy Together

From age three until I was 15, I went to a Convent school in my hometown, Alor Setar. There, both nuns and lay teachers taught me and the few other Muslim girls in the school, perhaps four or five in each class. As far as I know, every single one of them has remained Muslim to this day.

Our school building had a large cross on the roof and photos of Jesus on the walls. At school assembly we listened quietly as other students sang the Lord's Prayer. The nuns were covered head to toe in white and we liked some and feared others, because of their strictness in class. But mostly we were used to them and didn't have much curiousity about their lives.

We did not, however, grow up totally devoid of our own religion. We had compulsory *ugama* classes and on Saturdays we had Qur'an-reading classes. This was in addition to whatever classes our own parents might arrange for us at home. Nobody ever accused us of being less than regular Muslims, with less religious education than those who went to other schools.

And we got on with everyone. If I went to a birthday party at a non-Muslim friend's home, they made sure the food was halal. During Ramadan we still went to the canteen, but simply did not eat. None of us looked in envy – or resentment – at our friends eating. For that month, that was just the way things were.

I don't remember that we had to be protected from the sight or smell of food. Our parents had taught us that what fortified us on those hot days was our faith and our *niat* or intention to fast. Nor do I remember any of our friends trying to tempt us into breaking our fast by dangling food in front of us. I wish I could recall, however, what we did on the days when we couldn't fast. Did we simply go to the canteen and eat?

Could it be that in the years since I was a child, despite being subjected to more religious education, our faith is on more shaky ground than before? That it needs to be protected by indestructible walls built by the state because none of us can be trusted to believe on our own? Today, everything is apparently a threat to our faith, from yoga, to dressing in non-gender-specific ways, to seeing people eat when we can't. Nobody has any faith in faith anymore.

Fasting, for example, is hard only for the first few days. After the body and, more importantly, the mind, adjusts, life goes on as normal. There is no necessity to constantly guard against temptation unless we want to imply that we are weak creatures and it won't take much to make us fall off the wagon, so to speak.

There is therefore no need for the astonishing amount of grumpiness from all sides this Ramadan. Instead we should be endeavouring to make things light and easy for everyone, do charitable works and bring people together. Yet we see the opposite happening, whipped up by some of our leaders including religious ones who really should know better.

I think it is time we built up a resistance to the false causes that our leaders sometimes impose on us. On a day-to-day basis, we all get along, just as we did in my childhood. Yet things have also changed a lot and it is understandable that many of us get frustrated and furious with it.

But as that old adage goes, 'don't get mad, get even'. We should get even by resisting being manipulated into the fears that our leaders want us to feel. We should refuse to fall for any of the games that they play, which result mostly in making us feel more angry and fearful. We have to stop falling for ploys that divide us and resist by coming closer together to be more united.

There are plenty of ways of coming together if only we thought more creatively. This week, many of us Malaysians of every race and religion got together to spend one day of fasting together. Muslims who are fasting anyway reached out to their non-Muslim friends to share in either having the pre-fast meal or in the breaking of the fast together. Non-Muslims joined in fasting to experience what it feels like to not have any food or water from sun-up to sundown.

It is when we share an experience together that we are brought closer together. Today there are so many ways in which we are far apart, that we don't understand one another anymore.

We need to take action to change that. We need to resist.

*10 August 2013*

# Lessons from Cairo

I watched an extraordinary video the other day. In it, the imam of the Omar Makram mosque in Cairo, Egypt went with a delegation of 1000 from his congregation to attend Christmas service at Qasr Al-Dubarah Church, also in Cairo. Invited to speak, the imam sounded a clarion call for tolerance, respect, dignity, humanity and unity amidst difference and tumult. He also stated that Christians and Muslims must be united against any foreign and internal plots at increasing sectarianism or imposing Imperialist/ Colonialist designs on the Egyptian nation.

When I reposted this video on Facebook, people responded with delighted surprise, both Muslims and those of other faiths. Obviously we are all hungry for positive actions and messages like this. A group called MyJihad, which aims to reclaim the word 'jihad' to mean a personal journey and goal to do something good, first posted the video and at the end of it stated that their jihad was to build bridges between faiths.

It struck me that in the past few years when mutual suspicion and mistrust has increased between Malaysians of different faiths, very little has been done to build bridges and create peace. Everyone, especially politicians and religious officials with a political bent, seem keener on burning bridges instead. Each day another hurtful word is said, another suspicion aroused, another seed of mistrust sowed. It is only because ordinary Malaysians are far more sensible than their leaders that there has been so little violence, unlike say, in places like Pakistan. For that we have to be thankful, yet it doesn't take much, if one were so determined, to build up the seeds into a many-branched tree of hatred.

Not only are bridges being set alight between faiths but also within faiths. Those of us who want to be more respectful, conciliatory and generous are told that we are at risk of losing our faith. Yet in this video, here was an imam, educated in the venerable institution of Al-Azhar, who walks into a mosque, embraces his Christian brothers and states that it's his Islamic duty to be kind and neighbourly to them. He stresses that what Egypt needs now more than ever is unity between all her people, regardless of faith or creed, because they have so much to do the right the wrongs of the past, and repair the damage done by years of misrule.

It struck me that unity is also what Malaysians need: all of us, not just some. Once upon a time we stood firm against attempts by colonialists to divide and rule us. So must we do so again now.

We must therefore find ways to reach out to each other in peace. And I know lots of people have great ideas about how to do this, at neighbourly and community levels which is where it is most needed.

But the idea that struck me most while watching this video is one that seems to be the most obvious. Just as we have twinning of cities in Malaysia with cities around the world, why can't we have twinning of places of worship? Why can't a mosque and a church pair up and do things together? For example, they could, like the imam of the Omar Makram mosque and the pastor of the church, visit each other especially on special occasions. At other times, they could do *gotong royong* at each other's premises or have family days. In this way the congregation of the mosque and the congregation of the church could build a relationship with each other to not only understand each other better but also to build that bridge of trust and friendship we so badly need.

Imagine if Masjid Negara twinned with St John's Cathedral in Kuala Lumpur? What a beautiful example that would set! And maybe the imam could be asked to speak at the cathedral and the archbishop could be asked to speak at Masjid Negara? The day that happens I think I would cry, just like I cried the time I heard a Muslim imam recite the Al-Fatihah at the cathedral in Perth on the 10th anniversary of 11 September. There is nothing more moving that when you realise that we are all one people on this earth.

But I'm sure it's not going to happen because some people are determined to stress that they are superior to everyone else. Even though in the world today we are far behind everyone else in innovation, in creativity and in development. Our tiny little kampung seems to be all that matters to them.

Isn't it odd that those who think they are above everyone else have the smallest minds and hearts?

*17 January 2013*

# Bridge-Builders

They say fact is often stranger than fiction. Well, real life can often be better than slogans.

Long before we had this slogan about all being one, Malaysians already were. We went about our lives familiar with diversity, used to being citizens of many different hues. I suppose it's true when we say that we are not in fact a racist people, it's just that when something happens – an economic crisis, political insecurity – we express ourselves through racist behaviour. In Jared Diamond's book *Collapse: How Societies Choose to Fail or Succeed*, he shows how interracial or inter-tribal conflict often arises out of some economic issue, over land, food or some other ingredient essential to survival.

But the point is, when everything is going fine, people are not really racist and would probably remain so, even in troubled times, if opportunists did not stir things up. After all, it is as much a choice to explain things through economics as it is through a racist lens.

I for one generally believe that our people are essentially good, especially if left alone. For so long we have managed to live together quite happily, regardless of race or religious differences. And we have numerous real-life examples to prove it.

A friend was telling me about a family he met in Sabah that comprises a brother who is a Christian priest and a sister who is an ustazah. Both had made conscious choices to take these paths in life, and they remain loving siblings. In Sabah and Sarawak, it is not a situation that anybody bats an eyelid at.

In the Peninsula, in urban areas, I think there are many more of these mixed families than we really know. While it may be unusual to find such a situation among siblings, it is not unusual inter-generationally. That is, the parents may be of one religion and the children another. Nor would it be unusual among cousins and in-laws. I know one family where each daughter married a Christian, a Muslim and a Jew respectively. Thus their children would all be cousins of different religions. Last I heard, it wasn't an issue.

When I worked in HIV too, neither race nor religion was an issue in our everyday work. Since we were dealing with a virus that doesn't care what anyone believes in, neither could we discriminate against anyone if we wanted to be effective. We are all human with a common enemy. It did not make any sense to fight it individually in our own little corners.

I know of one story that truly illustrates how Malaysians can be caring without looking at people's race or religion. It also shows how the lack of political interference can allow people to be easily humane and compassionate.

Several years ago our army and police peacekeepers in Timor Leste befriended some orphans and took their orphanage under their wing. In the course of this, our medical corps realised that some of these orphans were in dire need of medical treatment that could not be found in that very poor country. So they arranged for them to be flown to Malaysia and, one by one, each got the treatment they needed and most of them recovered very well.

Today, 12 of the original 17 are still here studying because the

Malaysians who cared for them realised that for them to have any chance at all in life, they had to be educated here. And here's the best thing of all: these orphans are being looked after by a whole array of Malaysians who have simply ignored any racial or religious differences in order to do the best they can for these kids.

Timorese are very devout Catholics but the Army and police personnel who have been looking out for them are mostly Muslim. They organised their medical treatment and since they have been living here, often take them out for treats, invite them for Hari Raya open houses and lavish much affection on them. Additionally, a group of ladies from a Buddhist society helps to fund their groceries while others from various religious and social backgrounds assist in fundraising for their schooling and other daily needs. A local doctor – Muslim – lets them stay in a house he owns rent-free and doesn't fuss when they hang up religious pictures or builds a nativity scene at Christmas.

Every time I visit, my heart swells with pride at how generous and hospitable Malaysians have been towards these kids. Not only are these orphans getting a school education, they are also learning that people of different races and religions can live in peace together and not have to descend into civil war like their home country did.

It is possible to be bridge-builders. As long as we don't listen to politicians.

*16 February 2013*

# Fostering Unity through Fasting

First of all, let me wish everyone a Selamat Hari Raya Aidil Fitri, *maaf zahir batin*.

This year, the idea of forgiveness seems more poignant than ever, given the rancorous Ramadan we just had. I don't recall a month more full of anger and tension than this year's fasting month, ironic given that it is a month when believers are supposed to exercise restraint not only from food but also in thought, word and deed.

But the beginning of the month of Shawwal gives us an opportunity to press the reset button. We ask for forgiveness from our parents, family and friends for whatever wrongs big or small we may have done them in the past year including harsh words and rash deeds, and we forgive those who may have wronged us as well.

I was quite touched reading on Facebook the many status updates asking for forgiveness at Hari Raya by and from Muslims and non-Muslims alike. Malaysians seem to understand the spirit of the Raya season very well, regardless of their religion.

In fact in spite of the many upsetting events during Ramadan, there was still much that we can celebrate as Malaysians. One was the #Fast4Malaysia event organised by some friends of mine and me to foster unity through a common experience: fasting. On that one day, 31 July, non-Muslim Malaysians all over the country and even overseas fasted in solidarity with Muslims to understand what it feels like to not have any food or water from dawn to dusk.

About 60 of us woke up at 4.30 am to gather at a 24-hour eatery in Bangsar to have *sahur*, the pre-fast meal. Many of us knew one another but it was heartening to see people we didn't know join in. One young Chinese man came alone and was immediately invited by a young Malay family to sit with them. Another young woman drove all the way from Shah Alam to join in. Two Indian women happened to walk in the same restaurant without knowing what was happening but decided to join in when they learnt why we were there.

There was a sense of camaraderie among us that was truly unifying. Some first-timers were nervous about how they would cope but everyone else assured them it would be fine. All day on social media such as Twitter, people encouraged each other. Many young Muslims were thrilled and fascinated that their non-Muslim friends were joining them in the fast that day and gave many tips on how to manage the hunger. Non-Muslims chatted all day about their experience. They uploaded photos of what they ate at *sahur* and then later on photos of themselves breaking the fast with family and friends. Some people organised special *buka puasa* gatherings at home, in their offices and restaurants. Many blogged about their experience which was overwhelmingly positive. One teacher was at first greeted with incredulity by her fasting students which then became respect that she was joining them for the day. There were even some who continued to fast even after 31 July because they enjoyed the experience.

Even overseas Malaysians joined in. New Zealand was the first to *sahur* and break fast while Norway was the last. Thus we were connected through this experience not only with our immediate friends and family but also with those overseas, Malaysians linking hands around the world.

It's a pity that such a unifying event got so little coverage from the mainstream media and no mention at all from our leaders except for a few young Opposition politicians. Perhaps they should look up the #Fast4Malaysia Tumblr site to see how civil society can unite Malaysians in the sort of organic way that politicians cannot. There were no financial inducements, no sponsorship, no T-shirts involved. People went Dutch at *sahur* and *buka puasa* although some generous people hosted meals in their homes for their friends. Many made new friends along the way.

The main outcome was something no politician nor even religious leader could have engendered, mutual respect. Non-Muslim Malaysians, having fasted themselves, renewed their respect for their Muslim fellow citizens who do this for a whole month each year. Muslim Malaysians in return gained a new respect for their non-Muslim compatriots for attempting something which they had no obligation to perform. Both sides experienced something very precious for one another, empathy.

Of course, as is typical, there were detractors and cynics. Some questioned why fasting should be the experience we used, seeing it as an attempt to impose one religion's obligation over non-adherents. This was an ironic question given that the organisers came from all faiths. But we simply took the opportunity of Ramadan to respond to the many upsetting events during the month. If anyone has other creative ideas that can also unify people in the same way at other times of the year, then they should also do it. God knows we need many of these.

Many asked if we would do this again next year and every

year. The answer is we don't know. This was an attempt at uniting Malaysians at a time when there was much that was (and still is) divisive. We hope that there will be no more need for it in the future. But if there is, then we might. Or we might think of something else we can do that can bring us all together.

Ultimately it is a citizen initiative to bring peace at a time when our leaders fail us. And the more they fail us, the more ordinary Malaysian citizens need to find creative ways to keep us together.

Salam.

*17 August 2013*

# A Lesson in Real Harmony

When I was a little girl in Alor Setar, I thought that Malaya did not extend any further than my home state. I did eventually learn that in fact it was much bigger when we visited my grandparents in Kuala Lumpur. But for a long time my child geographical imagination was severely limited.

As an adult, of course, I have been all over the country. And despite being a pretty small one, there are distinct differences in environment, atmosphere and attitudes in different parts of the country, not to mention different dialects and foods. There is enough variety already within Peninsular Malaysia without us even experiencing what is on offer over the water, in Sabah and Sarawak. It is this diversity that makes our country wonderful.

Recently I was invited to Kuching to speak to some young people about social media and whether it contributes to social cohesion. I always jump at the chance to cross the water and it was a bit of a shock to realise that I hadn't been to Kuching for some five years. Besides the many culinary joys to be found there, it is always interesting to check out what Sarawakians are up to.

My hosts were two NGOs, Angkatan Zaman Mansang (AZAM) and the Islamic Information Centre (IIC), both, coincidentally, run by women. AZAM was set up 30 years ago to do development work among Sarawakians. Today they focus a lot on youth and support young people to do many things including volunteering to bridge the gap between urban and rural youth.

The IIC is only five years old but it was set up with some particular missions in mind. The first is to educate Muslims about Islam, the second is to educate non-Muslims about Islam and the third and most interesting of all, is to educate Muslims about other faiths. Muslims make up only 30% of Sarawak's population so it would be difficult to avoid other faiths in daily life. So IIC set out to build relationships between the different faiths so that they may understand each other better.

The Centre itself strives architecturally to be inclusive, borrowing elements from the housing styles of different ethnic groups in Sarawak including the Iban, Bidayuh, Orang Ulu, Malay and Chinese. Their surau holds Friday prayers in English and provides translations in various local languages so that no one feels alienated in those surroundings. Their resource centre contains many books on religion, particularly Islam, but their CEO was very proud to inform me that it contains a Bible as well.

Besides talks and panels for Muslims on Islam, they also often hold talks for non-Muslims on various aspects of the faith. And to educate Muslims about other faiths, they take groups of Muslims to visit other houses of faith to learn about them. Last year they organised a forum with AZAM on fasting, and how it is found in every religion.

This year's forum on social media was organised by both NGOs in the Christian Ecumenical Worship Centre and was attended by young people of every faith, including a visiting group of Muslim students from a public university in the Peninsula. Everyone was very relaxed, ate lunch together and the programme was designed so that those who had to go off to Friday prayers had ample time to get to the mosque.

While such a forum may have raised eyebrows in the Peninsula, or may even not have been organised out of fears of vocal criticism from certain parties, these types of events are not at all unusual for Sarawak. Sarawakians are used to living with such religious diversity and have no time for the sort of angst that we over here have. Some families have members of different faiths, so excluding some people from family events and festivities is simply not an option.

I listened with astonishment to the big-heartedness of the local religious authorities. For instance, every year at the Maal Hijrah (Muslim New Year) celebrations, alongside the usual Muslim recipients of the Tokoh Maal Hijrah awards, there is always a non-Muslim one, recognised for his or her efforts to foster better relations between the different faith communities. What's more, the Maal Hijrah parade also includes a contingent of non-Muslims. For someone from KL, used to the ever greater segregation on the basis of religion, this information was jaw-droppingly awesome.

But it is also sad to think of such harmony as being unusual. Once upon a time it was not uncommon either in our part of the country. We respected and lived with each other and did not claim names and beliefs to be exclusive to us.

But with changing attitudes, I feel as if I need to go to Kuching just to breathe.

*9 November 2013*

# Tackling the Trust Deficit

Much to my surprise, I was appointed to the National Unity Consultative Council (NUCC) last week. I would be lying if I said that I didn't have plenty of trepidation when I was asked just a few days before the launch to sit on this Council. Did it mean I have to tone down this column for instance?

But I felt a bit reassured when I saw some of the names that had been appointed, specifically the younger people there. To be sure, there are not enough women there (only six) and it could do with more really young people, those in their twenties and thirties. There is only one Opposition MP on it and we hope that the still-vacant spots in the lineup can be filled with more.

Of course the cynicism started almost as soon as the news got out. Many of us on the NUCC had already predicted that. Several of us mentioned the 'trust deficit' among the public for anything the government does and gave some reasons for why this was so. This is probably going to be our biggest obstacle, establishing our credibility to do what we are tasked to do which is to work out ways in which we can restore unity to our increasingly polarised country.

To do that, we have to be upfront and clear about what is causing the polarisation. Several of us on the Council are keen to do that and, indeed, have said that if we cannot be very frank, then there is no point in doing this. We were assured that we could be as frank as we want. We were also clear that we want to keep the process an open one. Hence those of us who have Twitter followers could follow what we were talking about in real time.

Indeed one of our first suggestions was that the NUCC should be on social media, with a Facebook page and Twitter account. This way we can hear people's views directly, besides the face-to-face meetings I believe are in the offing.

I can only speak for myself but I think for this Council to work, it needs to do so in very different ways from any other similar bodies. It needs to innovate and be pro-active. Personally, I would have liked there not to have been a president and deputy president appointed already, with all due respect to the current ones. It would have been great if we either elected among ourselves who would chair, or chose the less-obvious people to chair. That would immediately set it apart and break the normal protocol of doing things. Perhaps it's my NGO background where we always try to operate more democratically, but I think if we did things differently we might make some progress on that trust deficit.

We haven't had a real formal meeting yet but I'm hoping another NGO tradition can be transplanted to this. And that is, from the outset to get members to introduce themselves and state how they saw the workings of this Council and what they hope it will achieve. We are a diverse group so it cannot be assumed that we all know each other. And more importantly, we need to know that we are all on the same page and want to achieve the same goal, unity. To me, the first thing we should do is establish that this Council will operate in a democratic way and because we are all going to roll up our sleeves to work, then we should all be treated equally. All protocol should be set aside.

The expectations on us are high, perhaps too high. Unity is

not just a goal but a process so all we can do in our two years is to set Malaysians back on the road to the togetherness we used to have. It is ludicrous to think we would have all the answers in six months as some have suggested. If we can do one or two things that work, then I think we will build the confidence that it can be done.

So I think at this early stage, there is still some hope. I'm grateful that many people have kindly given the thumbs up to my appointment. But it's an awesome responsibility. Still I think at least we will give it a go and if we fail, it won't be for want of trying. I always believe that you never really lose if you are sincere and willing to work hard.

2014 is round the corner and after a difficult rancorous year, perhaps we need to put aside our misgivings and cynicism and be optimistic. Positivity begets positivity, God willing.

*7 December 2013*

# The Year of the Malaysian Citizen

I was afraid that this first column of the year would be a depressing and doleful one. 2014 was remarkable for its sheer awfulness, with not one but three plane accidents, the worst floods in our history and any amount of angst among our people due to the words and actions of various groups. Will 2015 be better or worse?

But for every action, there is a reaction and happily these reactions have also been unexpected and gratifying. In January, when a church was a possible target of violence, a group of people turned up to give out flowers to churchgoers and did much to ease the tension of that day. That was the birth of a group called Malaysians for Malaysia (M4M) that set out to promote unity and harmony among their fellow citizens. M4M then went on to organise the Walks in the Park in several cities that gave Malaysians the opportunity to simply gather and do things together.

When MH370 and MH17 happened, M4M was on hand to unite Malaysians with the Walls of Hope that allowed thousands of Malaysians and others to pour out their grief and hopes for the safety of the passengers of the former and prayers for the souls of the passengers of the latter.

M4M is certainly not the only group that sprang up to bring Malaysians together, not just in grief, but also in voluntarism. When there was a threat to shut down soup kitchens, KLites banded together to keep them going and even started new ventures to support the existing ones. Various individuals and groups have formed to do all sorts of charity work to help the poor, the marginalised, disabled and even animals. Civil society has stepped up and is going from strength to strength, a healthy sign.

Then when the worst floods ever in our history turned several states into exact replicas of countries far less developed than us, with people stranded and starving, Malaysians truly showed how generous and kind they can be. Collection centres for relief goods were set up in various neighbourhoods and when the calls for volunteers spread through social media, dozens showed up. I visited one and was truly moved and heartened by not only the number of people lending their time and energy to the effort to pack and send off the goods but by how diverse they were. They were young, old, male, female and represented every ethnic group including expats. And they worked side by side and took instructions from supervisors cheerily.

There are even people who have organised convoys of cars and trucks to try and reach the stranded folks on the east coast with tons of food and other essentials. Nobody told them to do it, nobody ever paid them to do it. They just did it because their fellow citizens were suffering and this was the right thing to do. You have to wonder where those self-proclaimed champions of race and religion are in these times and what they would say about these multiracial multireligious efforts to send aid to flood victims.

Indeed one of the happiest things that has happened in 2014 is the emergence of voices calling for more common sense in the way we discuss things in our country. The Group of 25* has been a pleasant surprise and has inspired more people to speak out against extremists and racists. Young people especially have welcomed this new development, having previously despaired of a positive future in this country. They have responded by organising petitions and writing articles of support for the G25, most notably by a multiracial group of 33 prominent citizens and a group of young Islamic Studies graduates from Middle Eastern universities. These developments have really brought hope to many concerned Malaysians.

So perhaps when you look at it from this perspective, things were not so bad after all in 2014, despite the major tragedies. While we mourn those we lost, and sympathise with those who are suffering in the floods right now, we can also rejoice in the fact that 2014 was really the year that The Malaysian Citizen showed that their natural kindness and generosity enabled them to respond much faster and more efficiently than any politician can. This is truly community leadership at its best.

For 2015, perhaps we can put our hopes in The Malaysian Citizen and therefore be more optimistic about the coming year. Their sense of unity that arises out of a sense of fairness is fully developed. What The Malaysian Citizen has shown is that there is no law needed to foster unity. They will unite naturally against suffering and injustice. The only proviso is obvious: keep the politicians out of it.

*1 January 2015*

---

\* The Group of 25 (G25) is a group of influential Malays, mostly retired senior civil servants, who in December 2014 published an open letter calling for open discourse to reclaim Malaysia from growing extremist religious and racial elements.

# Moderate Malaysians

Of late there's been a lot of talk about how moderate Malaysians need to rise up and speak up against the extremists in our country. While this is certainly a much-needed call, we find that definitions tend to get in the way. For example, everyone denies being an extremist and claims to be moderate. It seems that in this country, as long as you don't pick up a gun and go and shoot someone, you're not an extremist. Those who certainly spout violent and hate-filled language are not yet defined as extremist even though their talk may spur some followers to do the worst imaginable one day. After all if they can make the effort to go join a band of brigands who have no qualms about chopping off heads and burning people alive, why wouldn't they be as motivated at home?

If everyone is now claiming to be moderate, there is a need to further define what would be the true characteristics of such a person. There are indeed differences between true moderates and those merely pretending to be one.

For one thing, a true moderate respects another person's point of view even when those views are patently abhorrent. For a moderate, freedom of speech and expression is a very important value. A non-moderate however can barely tolerate any viewpoint that is contrary to theirs and would rather they were not allowed to speak at all. If they had to engage with another group, it would only be to convince the others that they are wrong and must immediately convert to the non-moderate perspective. No middle ground there.

Secondly, the non-moderate believes that there needs to be a law for everything. Without punitive measures, they believe that people will simply all go wild and do all sorts of crazy things. For example, according to them, people cannot be trusted not to walk the streets naked if there is no law against it.

True moderates on the other hand trust that an average human being in our country has quite a bit of common sense and will not simply be anti-social just because they can. Malaysians, like most Asians, do care what people think of them and that acts as a major deterrent to any sort of bizarre behaviour. For example, gathering a large group to go and shake posteriors in front of someone's house cannot, by any measure, be considered a common sense act and therefore anyone who does that cannot rightly be called moderate.

Moderates tend to speak in a careful way. Every word is considered well before spoken or written and tends not to be overblown or exaggerated because that would be immodest and therefore immoderate. On the other hand, a non-moderate person tends to shoot his mouth off, verbally and in writing, refuse to apologise, organises people to show support with unoriginal slogans and then sits back while his boss gives a lame excuse for his bad behaviour. It stands to reason that many non-moderates are a bit lacking in the integrity department.

It might be fair to say that maturity is also a hallmark of the moderate person. The moderate person knows that you don't need to comment about every single thing simply because you cannot be an expert in everything. You especially cannot spend all your time making police reports about everything other people say and do, not least because this may give the impression that you have plenty of time on your hands and have no need to earn a living like other people.

The non-moderate however thinks nothing of filing multiple police reports in a single day on anything that comes to mind that they can spin as insulting to themselves. In this way they keep our already harried police force busy trying to work out what precisely their complaints are and not out chasing all manner of crooks including those stealing public money. In fact perhaps we can define extremists as those who spend their time wasting taxpayers' money by making all sorts of facetious police reports, especially those that are not actually crimes. And we should also ask why they have the luxury of spending all day at police stations, sometimes wearing outrageous costumes, without the need to have any sort of job. How DO they pay for their daily nasi lemak?

There may be other ways to differentiate the true moderate from the false one. There aren't, for example, many publicity hounds who can convince anyone they are actually moderate in their views. They understand very well that extreme views make for good TV. So virtually anyone you see too often in the mainstream media is probably suspect.

Meanwhile the rest of Malaysia is trying to get by on their increasingly less-moderate incomes.

*12 February 2015*

# We Should Be Ashamed

Sometimes we need to look at our country from a long distance to truly see it as it is. I have been travelling for the past two weeks and while it is nice to totally switch off news from home, occasionally I can't help it. And predictably enough there is hardly ever news that makes me homesick. Instead there is only news that makes me sick at heart.

The whole resort surau issue* blew up right after I left and, honestly, reading about it from afar makes me want to shake my head at the ridiculous lengths our politicians will go to to supposedly garner popularity.

I won't repeat the numerous sensible arguments so many have put forward against taking punitive action against the resort manager for what is at worst a naïve mistake. When people have apologised, magnanimity requires that we accept it. Not accepting apologies reeks of arrogance. After all, even God accepts those who repent.

In fact, the one striking thing about the recent many occurrences of the ease of offendedness is not only the sudden thin-skinness of mostly politicians and religio-politicians but also the actual audience for this. When it comes to religion, we are always exhorted to do everything for God. Even given that some people actually think getting offended is a good thing, I have to ask: are we doing this for God or simply other human beings, especially those whose votes we need in coming elections? If it is the latter, then we are already wrong.

And if it is the former, then why would Almighty God not only choose to speak through the minister of home affairs but choose the taking away of permanent residency as His chosen form of punishment?

Nor is the destruction of places of worship something that is sanctioned by the God some of us purport to represent. As many have pointed out, places of worship often go through various incarnations. The Kaaba itself was once a temple of idolatory until the Prophet Muhammad pbuh cleansed it of its idols. Today it is Islam's holiest site. If the Kaaba can be so easily converted as a holy place from one faith to another, what more a humble hotel surau?

Honestly, from afar, our politicians and their band of followers simply look stupid. There are far more important things to worry about than whether rooms can be used for one faith or another, or what one calls God or whether everyone fits into one uniform faith box or not. All over the world people are dying from hunger and war. How does the destruction of one surau help them?

In the UK, everywhere I go, I see posters gently requesting people to donate to causes in developing countries, to help people have clean water, simple medical treatment or for children to go to school. The football association has just started a campaign for tougher penalties against racism, sexism and homophobia. These are all positive things to do because those who are voiceless and powerless will feel more protected.

In contrast, in our country, every day we only see more calls for the voiceless and the powerless to be even more marginalised and discriminated against. And the worst thing is, not only do we think this the right and – gallingly – the religious thing to do, but we are actually proud of it.

If we only read our religious books, then we would know that we should actually be ashamed.

*31 August 2013*

* A controversy in August 2013 caused by a resort in Johor allowing Buddhists to meditate in its Muslim prayer room. The surau was later demolished as a result of orders from the Johor State Government and Kota Tinggi Municipal Council. The resort staff member who allowed the Buddhists to use the surau was Syed Ahmad Salim, a Singaporean with permanent resident status in Malaysia. He was detained by the police following the incident for four days, investigated for allegedly defiling a place of worship, and released. No charges were brought against him but his permanent resident status was revoked by the Ministry of Home Affairs for the reason that he was insensitive to Muslims and Islam.

# The Value of Dignity

One of the things that we try to impart to our children is the value of human dignity; we try and teach them to respect others, never to shame others in public and to always conduct ourselves with decorum. Our pity is often cast on those whose lives have fallen apart and have to bear the indignities that society can wreak on the indigent and the ill.

We know that the importance of respecting a person's dignity is also tied to respecting their bodily integrity. Hence our concern – some would say, obsession – with the way people, especially women, are dressed. The ostensible reason is that it protects a person's physical integrity. A dignified person is therefore a whole person, respected and respectful.

Imagine therefore my horror and shock at a story of an ustazah in a school who, disbelieving her female students who said they could not pray because they had their period, decided to check their underwear to see if they were telling the truth.

It must be a special kind of sick sadist that thinks that checking another person's underwear is a viable way of carrying out their duties. It is a blatant abuse of power over those who are unable to refuse the command. Mothers rarely ask to look at their very young daughters' underwear except with very good reason such as if they suspect they are ill. Why then does a teacher, who otherwise has no business to touch the bodies of our children, feel she can do this with impunity?

Imagine the effect it will have on the students. It is bad enough not to be believed but to be violated in this way must surely have an effect on their self-esteem. Do we not care if we bring up children with low self-esteem or is that the idea, to create a whole generation of subservient girls? More insultingly, it is done in the name of religion.

It just points to the sheer ludicrousness of public ritual as an indicator of piety. I don't know what KPI the ustazah had that she had to ensure that every single girl under her charge prayed every day. Yet for all the praying, which presumably she does too, she still could not trust her own charges. If they say they cannot pray that day, then really she should just trust them and leave it in the hands of the Almighty.

Apparently this sort of thing is not uncommon in our schools and even in Muslim schools elsewhere. A friend told of how when she was in school, girls had to indicate on a chart when they had their period. If their period lasted more than 15 days, then this was cause for speculation that they were lying and therefore liable to be subject to punishment for not praying.

I have to wonder what punishment is reserved for boys who try to excuse themselves from prayers since there are no similar indicators for them. Should girls be punished merely because of biology?

The reaction of most of my friends who heard this story is that the parents of the girls should sue the teacher and the school. Schools are after all meant to be spaces that are safe for our children. Safety does not just mean physical safety but safety from the sort of mental abuse that this sort of physical 'inspection' causes.

But the chances are that the parents won't. Firstly, they are likely to feel embarrassed about the whole thing and secondly, who are they to dispute a teacher, and a religious teacher at that, who has power over their child for most of the day? They are also likely to be shamed for not keeping tabs on their daughters' prayer schedules themselves. In other words, such abusive teachers are likely to carry on this behaviour knowing that nothing much will happen to them.

What do we teach our children when we behave like this? We teach them that power over someone weaker is everything, that the powerful can do anything but they can especially humiliate a powerless person. We teach our children that their bodies are not theirs, and yet at the same time we scold and punish them if they allow the 'wrong' people to touch them. Is an ustazah, even if she is of the same sex, the right person? Some people will say she was only looking and not touching. That's splitting hairs, really.

It is things like this that make parents lose trust in our schools and our teachers. Schools are where our children should be able to grow as human beings, to fulfil their potential to be contributing members of society.

Instead we are turning them into humiliated people who may well turn into future abusers themselves.

*14 September 2013*

# Where's the Justice Now?

Whenever Islam is attacked for being violent and oppressive, many Muslims are quick to defend their religion as one of peace. At each attack, the same words are trotted out as if these alone would be evidence of such truth. In fact very often the words are not enough because the actions that many Muslims do in the name of Islam are far from being peaceful or just. Worse still, that the injustices and violence are mostly inflicted on other Muslims.

How is it possible to classify the burning of houses of worship of other faiths, or the abuse, and sometimes killing, of people of other faiths or other Muslim denominations as peaceful? How do we classify the rape of Mukhtar Mai, the Pakistani woman given to another family because of an alleged wrong done by her brother, as just? Or, the shooting of Malalai Yousufzai?

Nearer home, how do we proclaim Islam a just religion when the poor disproportionately are unable to obtain justice in our courts, when women have to spend energy and money they don't have going in and out of court to get what is rightfully theirs and their children's from irresponsible husbands? What sort of justice is it when a woman who, fed up with the long-drawn-out process, insists that the court punish her by whipping her is seen as a good Muslim woman, while men who repeatedly ignore court orders are not seen as bad Muslim men?

What sort of justice is it that women are invariably blamed for all of society's ills but never men?

This week a gross act of injustice has been done by the Federal Territory shariah court to a young woman who had the misfortune of being female and Muslim when confronted by JAWI officials looking for someone to arrest*. They could not arrest her non-Muslim boss nor could they charge her employers. So they picked on her and subjected her to unabating harassment to this day.

Never mind that the civil courts found that JAWI had no right to raid the bookstore before the book they sought was even banned. Never mind that the civil courts lifted the ban on the book. If the conditions for her arrest no longer exist, it stands to reason that whatever charges against her must be withdrawn. After all, the courts have said that the book is not banned, therefore how can she be charged for selling a banned book?

Here is where hubris trumps justice. Instead of gracefully withdrawing the charges against her, JAWI did a duplicitous thing. In order not to be cited as being in contempt of the civil High Court's order to lift the ban, they said they respected the court's orders. But then they said that the shariah judge had the power to make his own judgment on the case. And he duly did, by refusing to withdraw the charge.

In what universe is this justice? In what world does this contribute to the image of Islam as a religion of justice and of peace? And what are the implications of this incredible judgment?

Firstly, it means that no bookstore, except perhaps those selling Islamic books, may employ any Muslim at all since they will be held responsible for the content of every single book in the inventory that may contradict Islamic teachings. Does this mean that all bookstores must now fire all their Muslim employees?

Secondly, what about other employers that may have in their

workplace things that are also considered unIslamic, such as alcohol? Does this now mean that no Muslim may be employed in hotels, restaurants, even on our national airline? At a time when jobs are already hard to come by, how do we help anyone with this ridiculous judgment?

And it's ridiculous because it makes no sense. The court session was only meant to be a formality to withdraw the charges against the woman, since logically speaking there is no reason to charge her. But the judge decided to prolong the case, make it even more controversial and perhaps even trigger a constitutional crisis. All for what purpose?

Meanwhile a young woman, who has worked hard to get to where she is, has to continue living with this charge over her head. That she has done so with great equanimity is testimony to her fortitude and courage. Or perhaps, as a Muslim she knows better this verse than the judge:

BEHOLD, God enjoins justice, and the doing of good, and generosity towards [one's] fellow-men; and He forbids all that is shameful and all that runs counter to reason, as well as envy; [and] He exhorts you [repeatedly] so that you might bear [all this] in mind. (Surah An-Nahl, Verse 90, translation by Muhammad Assad).

*12 October 2013*

*Borders bookshop manager Nik Raina Abdul Aziz was arrested and charged by JAWI in 2012 with selling a banned book, *Allah, Liberty and Love*, by Iranian author Irshad Manji. She was eventually granted a discharge not amounting to an acquittal by the Shariah High Court in February 2015.

# When the World Turns Upside Down

In recent times I have felt like Alice in Wonderland. In Lewis Carroll's tale, Alice slipped down a rabbit hole and suddenly the whole world is turned upside down. She either becomes too small or too big, and all the odd characters around her speak in riddles. The world of Wonderland is a very puzzling place.

The world I live in too has become a very puzzling place. Things have different meanings from what they used to and reason and logic are no longer what they were.

Once upon a time, being kind to others was a very good thing to be. We were taught by parents and teachers to be nice to others regardless of who they were, because how we behaved was a direct reflection of how we were brought up. We were also taught to be fair to others, to not take what was not ours and to be considerate to those who were older and wiser than us.

Today, we are told that while being kind is still a good thing, we have to mind who we are nice to. Being considerate and polite to some people is now considered a mortal sin simply because they believe in things differently from us. We cannot, for instance, wish that a dead person rests in peace because apparently having not believed in the same faith as we do, they cannot possibly have a peaceful afterlife. While in all likelihood the dead person will not know what we wished them, there is still the living family and loved ones to consider. Surely we should not add to their sorrow by wishing their deceased husband or father ill in the afterlife.

Not unless we want them to dislike us.

What was once just harmless common courtesy has now been poisoned by those with nothing better to do than to think of endless ways to be rude to others. Happiness today is defined by how many people you can make unhappy each day.

When we lost all those people in MH370, did anyone differentiate between which families they sent their sympathies to and which they didn't? Didn't that tragedy affect everybody equally? Aren't the families of MH370 now all forever linked to one another by this common disaster, regardless of who they are and where they come from? Yet the loss of one person to an equally tragic car accident (as well as his assistant) was treated as if it was cause for celebration. Where once people were mindful not to show their ill-feelings publicly, today it is advertised proudly. The world down that rabbit hole has come to the surface.

In a time not too far away, people thought that the cutting of hands and the stoning of humans were too uncivilised for a modern democratic country like ours. When some tried to introduce it, it was greeted with derision. Today even the most unlikely people are welcoming it, as if this is the answer to all our problems. Is it because people we admire because they have lots of money have now decided that they will impose such barbaric punishments on their citizens and non-citizens alike? For what reason do we admire this move when, apart from conspicious consumption, there is absolutely nothing else to say about that country? Why do we choose to ignore that this new 'justice system' exempts the elite from the same punishments they want to impose on everyone else?

Is that why our elite are also rushing to endorse this new move?

Because they know that it will not affect them at all, only those who are poor, marginalised and whom they dislike? What sort of society do we foresee when the poor are left crippled because they cannot afford to get justice from this system so many are now eager to introduce? If it is meant to be better than what we have now, what do these improvements look like? What, for example, would be the equivalent of the Domestic Violence Act in the hudud laws? Or will it be completely void because in a pure 'Islamic' state, men will be able to beat their wives with impunity?

Today, reason is being chiselled away daily to be replaced by religious gamesmanship, with no thought for what the consequences will be. Everyone is trying to outdo one another with ever more 'religious' pronouncements, even though so little of it makes any sense at all. Is a religious state merely about punishing people? How does such a state deal with practical issues like globalisation or climate change, or even more mundane domestic issues like our water woes, public transport or even education? Or is the answer simply to be like the Queen of Hearts and say 'Off with his head!'

*25 April 2014*

# We've Got Walking Time-Bombs

So we finally stepped over the line. When the first Malaysian suicide bomber died in Syria, we finally put to rest the idea that Malaysian Muslims would never do this. For so long, we have believed that suicide in itself is a sin and such drastic action is sinful because it harms and kills innocent people. But now these concepts seem not to hold water anymore.

In the age of social media, not only are our youth going off to fight wars in a foreign land, they are even boasting about it to all their friends back home via Facebook and Twitter. They need this self-advertising in order to ensure that everyone thinks of them as heroes and warriors, fighting for a cause that nobody really understands. After all, by joining ISIS, they are fighting other Muslims, not people of other faiths.

But why should we be surprised at this development? For the past year or so, Malaysian Muslims have been bombarded by propaganda against Shias in the mosques and in the media. Alleged Shias are arrested and few care what happens to them. Our home minister, never known to be a theologian, has even declared Shias unIslamic, something even the rabidly anti-Shia Saudis have never done. Shias make up only about 10% of the world's Muslims and even fewer in number in Malaysia compared to Sunnis.

Yet our IGP, another amateur theologian, insisted that if we do not control Shia activities in Malaysia, it 'could lead to militant activities. We do not want what happened in Syria, Iraq, Afghanistan and Pakistan to happen here, do we?' Well, he's wrong on two counts. The Malaysian militants going to fight with ISIS in Syria are all Sunni, and if Syria doesn't happen here, then they'll just go to Syria. If they survive, they'll eventually bring it home.

According to another Malaysian on a humanitarian mission to Syria who met one of these jihadists, 'Most of them who join are fanatics, *mat rempit*s, those without high education or were from problematic families. Some of them committed some big sin and were told that they could purify themselves by taking part in the jihad. They want a short cut to heaven.'

This is an important clue as to what drives these young men to join a war far away from home. When home is dull and problematic, a foreign war with the promise of heaven sounds infinitely more exciting. Getting heads broken at their motorbike races on Friday nights pales in comparison to actually holding an AK47 and killing another human being. Back home if you kill someone you might get punished for it. Here in Syria, you'll go to heaven. What could be better than that? Even the clothes are cooler.

If anyone is worried about this development, and they certainly should be, then the answer is to look at the state of our young men today, particularly the Muslim men at the bottom of the social scale. The ones who drop out of school early and face a future of either unemployment or menial work. The ones who take drugs in order to make their dull and bleak everyday lives slightly more interesting.

And we need to take some responsibility for these young men. We've been telling them that as Malay Muslim men, they are superior to everyone else and entitled to everything in this country. Yet when they fail to attain any of these, when this so-called entitlement only goes to those with better connections than them, we discard and neglect them and call them names like 'rempit'. We prohibit them from being anything but what we want them to be, and while we sneer at them, we also glorify and romanticise the violence in their lives through movies and novels. The hero apparently always gets the girl, even if he has to rape her first.

But in real life, this doesn't happen. The girls would rather they had a good job and a decent car. As drug-ridden fishermen or mechanics, they'll never earn enough to win the girls of their dreams. That rage sometimes leads them to take it out on the nearest girls, the ones in their own villages. Why not? After all, society will always blame the girls anyway.

It is likely these are the types of young men who wind up wooed by jihadist recruiters with promises of adventure, excitement and a free pass to heaven where the best girls are waiting.

We are complicit in the wasted lives of these young men. We may wring our hands in disbelief now but we've been moulding them for this for years. Why should we be surprised now?

Maybe some deeper reflection on our responsibility is needed this Ramadan.

*4 July 2014*

# The Cult of Unthinking

There are times when I just want to give up. One of those times recently was when I saw a tweet calling on people not to buy the latest Proton model because its name supposedly signifies the one-eyed false Messiah.

I didn't know whether to laugh or cry. I have no idea whether it's a good car or not but I do know that the person who wrote the tweet not only has a poor command of English but has the sort of brain that sees evil under every rock. It's not a great brain admittedly but the owner of it seems not at all bashful about hiding that fact.

But more importantly this was yet another example of the Malaysian propensity to attach religious symbolism to everything. The foam of a café latte might conjure up a face and everyone assumes it must be someone important, because why would unimportant faces appear in milk froth? Parties, and indeed any form of fun, are the Devil's way of distracting us from turning ourselves into stultified robots. Why, even the delicious and undoubtedly sensual taste of ice cream is something to be wary of, especially when the ice cream comes with what might look like a religious symbol (if you had that turn of mind) on it.

What is it about us that we can't take something just for what it is? Why does everything have to be a conspiracy theory of some kind? Apparently we Asians (and Arabs and probably Africans too) are incapable of ever thinking for ourselves and therefore if we ever demand things like freedom of speech and other basic democratic freedoms, we must surely be manipulated by someone else. Never mind that we once fought for our independence without anyone else putting the idea in our heads.

It is a patronising and condescending not to mention racist attitude about our own kind. And it is really the upshot of an education system that is geared towards keeping our minds small, and an environment that downgrades science and scientific fact in favour of superstition, rumours, whims and gossip. Somehow using our brains has fallen into disfavour, while the wackiest ideas spread like wildfire.

I see endless bizarre stories being spread through social media that, were anyone inclined to pause and think for a bit, would not make sense to a rational mind. But then if we are constantly being told not to think, to accept that there are many things that simply have no explanation, why should we be surprised that people are constantly seeing shadows where there are none?

Not thinking leads people to support the idea that we have no choice in our lives. If we disapprove of a concert or an event, we do have the choice not to go to it, especially if we are required to buy tickets first. If someone puts a beer in front of us, we do have the choice not to drink it. As human beings with brains, we do have agency, meaning that we can make our own choices. We are not puppets controlled in such a way that we are unable to resist anything. This is the sort of thinking that blames victims for what happens to them. If we had no agency and therefore no choice, then how can we blame men for raping or killing? They apparently had no choice but ironically the victim could choose not to put themselves in such situations.

It's funny how we always seem to think that we have no choice when it comes to doing evil but plenty of choice to do good things that we then don't exercise. Doing good works is also something we can exercise our agency to do, or not. Yet nobody ever says they involuntarily did something good simply because someone put an orphan or a homeless person in front of them.

If we are religious and assume that we constantly have to guard against the Devil's evil influence, how is it that we are never appreciative of God's good influence over us to be kind and compassionate? Instead we sometimes even treat people inhumanely and kill innocent people supposedly in the name of the Divine. In fact we always also have a choice to do none of these, also in the name of the Merciful and Compassionate.

This cult of unthinking is based on the assumption that we must always submit to things we don't understand because we can never verify them. Yet we are given clear instructions: 'And never concern thyself with anything of which thou hast no knowledge: verily, [thy] hearing and sight and heart – all of them – will be called to account for it [on Judgment Day]!' (Chapter 17, verse 36, translation by Assad).

*10 October 2014*

# From Touch a Dog to How to Be an Adulterer

Last Sunday an extraordinary young man organised an extraordinary event. Having lived his life being afraid of dogs, he decided to overcome this fear, and help others to do the same, by inviting people to get to know some dogs. He got all the necessary permissions, promoted it and on the day, almost a thousand people, Muslims and non-Muslims turned up.

By all accounts the event was a success and people went away enlightened, and happy. Unfortunately among those whose role in life is seemingly to keep us all ignorant, there was great unhappiness. Who is this young man who could get so many people out of their beds on a Sunday morning? How come they all seem to be smiling and, goodness gracious, enjoying themselves?

Thus, to no one's surprise, they immediately started to condemn him and all those who took part in the event. Never mind that the intention of those who attended was to learn about one of God's own creatures and how to treat them kindly. The organisers had done everything right, including having someone give a talk on the Islamic viewpoint on dogs as well as having all the ingredients needed for the ritual cleansing after touching wet dogs. Yet this was not good enough for our authorities.

I often wonder if what bothers our 'religious' authorities most is not so much the actual religious ins and outs of any event or action, but anything that would challenge their so-called authority, and certainly anything that makes someone else popular. The organiser of the Touch a Dog event did not intend for the event to insult anyone. After all, those who felt uncomfortable about it can always stay home. I suspect that the response against the event only came when they realised that quite a lot of people turned up. They had probably assumed that few would because they thought everybody had already bought their so-called opinions against dogs. Lo and behold, about 500 or so Muslims did not!

Apparently coming together to learn about animals and how to be kind and compassionate towards them will lead everyone down the slippery slope to even more nefarious acts. I didn't realise that kindness is now considered despicable but then the world has turned upside down. What's next, the rabid types ask, Touch a Pig Day? Others ask if this will lead to How to Be An Adulterer classes, though I would suggest that we already have plenty of those.

How is it that nobody thinks that acts of kindness and compassion will lead to more acts of generosity and goodwill? If people can be kind to dogs, then we might put a stop to things like throwing stones at them or the abandoning of puppies. Where does it say that it is okay to beat or starve animals? And why should those who are kind to them be condemned? My aunt used to take in stray dogs and cats rather than allow them to be left to the elements. The couple in Kedah who cares for dogs, however, was forced to move*. Ignorance seems to lead to nothing but cruelty. Are we actually proud of that?

I believe that Malaysians, both Muslims and non-Muslims, are just dying for someone to tell them something positive, which is why they responded so well to Touch a Dog Day. We all know what the big sins are and we know how to avoid them. But we are so rarely told how to get along with one another, how to live in harmony with one another, as well as with other living things in our environment.

All we are getting is how to hate an ever-growing list of people and things. How much energy are we to spend on hate? And how does hating anything and everything make us happy and better Muslims? Why is it that if we are to hate anything, we are not encouraged to direct hatred towards the corrupt, the ignorant and the cruel? Why are we never taught to revile injustice, rather than revere it as some people in power do?

Chapter 5, verse 8 of the Qur'an says 'O YOU who have attained to faith! Be ever steadfast in your devotion to God, bearing witness to the truth in all equity; and never let hatred of anyone lead you into the sin of deviating from justice. Be just: this is closest to being God-conscious. And remain conscious of God: verily, God is aware of all that you do.' (Translation by Assad.)

If hatred can lead us to the sin of injustice, then perhaps it stands to reason that the opposite, love, can lead us to the virtue of justice. Isn't that what we should be striving for?

*23 October 2014*

* Pak Mie and Mak Intan, at the Pak Mie Animal Shelter, Tanjung Bendera, Alor Setar.

# Halal versus Haram Television Programmes

You can read very interesting things in the news these days, some of which can be rather puzzling. At a conference on entertainment and Islam recently, a paper presenter said that many people have asked him how to tell if a TV programme is threatening or not to their faith.

I really had to wonder who these people were and why this was such a problem. Most people can tell within five minutes of watching a programme whether it's any good or not. Perhaps it is harder to tell if an interesting programme, say about the mating habits of bees, will shake your faith but what most sensible people do is to see if it makes them feel uncomfortable or not. If it does, then their faith is probably shaky. And the most obvious thing to do, naturally, is to switch it off.

I don't particularly like scary horror-type programmes, not because I think they would shake my faith, but because I don't find them enjoyable. So I switch channels to something more innocuous like Downton Abbey. Apparently in Victorian times, nobody ever made any public displays of affection so I reckon that's pretty safe for anyone.

But the paper presenter actually spent a lot of time thinking about these questions from people presumably without on/off buttons on their TVs nor channel-changing remote controls. So he then proposed that all TV programmes should carry halal and haram certificates.

OK, all those who volunteer to certify the haram programmes, please put up your hands!

What would probably happen is that 90% of the programmes will wind up in one way or another with a haram certificate while the rest would be deemed kosher. That is probably because the criteria for halalness are going to be very strict and long. How long should the tudung be? How tight can her sleeves be? How many sequins is too much? Is that a hipster or a halal beard? These are all questions to be decided by arguably the least hip people in the country.

But the scenario that plays in my mind is this. Here is a Muslim household where the head of the family, a man of course, is sitting in front of the TV feeling somewhat guilty about the choice of channels he has before him. He thinks he should just watch the religious programmes but really he would rather watch the hot Indonesian or Latin American actresses on all those never-ending soap operas. But no matter what he does he keeps being tempted to switch back to those channels.

He sits there chained to his armchair unable to move from in front of the TV, hapless at all the choice in front of him. During the Olympics the problem is worst. There's women's beach volleyball, women's swimming, women's gymnastics. What threats to his faith!!

Of course women are not so threatened by this terrible dilemma because they are so busy cooking, cleaning, helping the kids do their homework that they simply have no time to watch the TV. Besides, they've already been warned that during the World Cup they are not to watch any matches because the sight of those nice athletic long legs might do something bad to their insides. Still, wives have been blamed too for not switching the channels for their husbands from women in swimsuits to women in hijab.

But the men, seated with their T-shirts pulled tight over their big nasi-lemak-filled bellies, are at real risk. They are helpless. They cannot get out of their seats and go do something else, like go for a walk, play with their kids, help their wives with the washing up. They are stuck and therefore their faith is endangered. Hence, the need to have a whole conference to discuss this.

Meanwhile there is a huge financial scandal that is threatening to turn the entire population into paupers, climate change is causing floods, mudslides and turning people out of their homes by the dozens, there are hungry and homeless people in our streets, more and more poverty in our faces today. And as I write this, a siege is ongoing in Sydney that means yet again Muslims are going to be stereotyped as terrorists.

But none of these are as important as which TV programmes will get us to heaven and which will not. And whose fault it is really for producing programmes which put us on the fast-track to hell.

I'm going to spend my time either reading, watching good dramas on TV or going out to visit friends for Christmas. In fact the only thing worth watching is actually my waistline.

Meanwhile may I wish everyone Merry Christmas and a new year that is more hopeful, joyful and peaceful than 2014 was!

*22 December 2014*

# A Step Closer to Barbarism

A staple of the news these days is the many barbaric acts of the group known as the Islamic State or ISIS in Syria. Every day we are treated to news of their threats as well as actual acts of murder and mayhem against every person or group they don't like. They particularly specialise in the most gruesome ways of killing people such as by beheading or burning them to death alive. And those are the lucky ones. Those left alive, especially women, are forced to endure the lifelong stigma of rape and abuse. Over here we widen our eyes in horror at such atrocities. Our officials are at pains to point out that these acts of barbarism are unIslamic and they have had significant success in arresting various people on their way to Syria to join IS. Sermons are written to impress on us that we should not participate in this violence because of the very real fear that some people may get such a taste for it over there that they may want to do the same back home.

But we seem to be missing something here. Nobody needs to actually go to the Middle East in order to become barbaric. Here at home we have moved one step closer to becoming very IS-like already. Regardless of whether we can actually implement any of these measures – amputations, floggings, stoning – the mentality is already implanted. All in the most official and 'democratic' way too.

If anyone has the temerity to protest any of it, why, out come the daggers! Thousands of fingers eagerly tap their keyboards to issue death or rape threats to anyone who has the courage to point out that the 'laws' we want so much to implement should be the least of our priorities. How can we have laws that require amputations for thieves when so many are in poverty? Why do we want to punish people in unQur'anic ways?

If IS does not exist in physical form in our country, it sure exists in the heads and fingers of so many of our people. Despite being followers of a religion that does not allow killing or any kind of injustice towards our fellow humankind, they think they are doing their 'religious' duty by doing exactly the opposite. Baying like a pack of hounds for blood, the mob descends on anyone who speaks out, especially if they are female and Muslim. To them, to think differently and to actually voice concerns is to deviate from the programme. We have to be like them, programmed to be obedient. And bloodthirsty.

If our authorities cannot see the connection between these acts of aggression towards those with different opinions and their futile attempts to stop people from joining IS, then they are either unintelligent or purposely blind. If IS is the nadir of a civilised society, then we are heading there, make no mistake.

Where are the voices to condemn IS? Instead we have so much illogical and ignorant thinking that one wonders if we should preserve those brains to be studied somewhere in the future when we hopefully regain our sanity. One person says we should look to Nigeria for the 'successful' implementation of hudud. I suppose that's why Nigeria is such a successful country that their citizens are all over the world trying to make money.

Another person suggests that we must be on the right track because we are neither IS nor 'liberal' so we must be nicely middling and moderate. Sermons blare this warped definition of moderate every Friday. If you're not with us, you're either a liberal or an IS bandit. I would rather be a liberal who cares when people receive death threats rather than a 'moderate' who keeps silent when citizens are faced with such violence. A truly moderate government protects its citizens from violence, rather than encourages it by saying nothing.

I would like to ask our prime minister one question: are some of us Malaysians worth less to him than others? If so, may we know which ones and why? Should the 'worthless' ones wear stars on their foreheads so that everyone knows who they are and can do what they want to them? If this differentiation is legal in the law, will our law enforcement officers stand by mute when something bad happens?

I fear for my country. We have so many good people in this land; kind, courteous and compassionate people. Unfortunately we have poor leaders, self-serving ones who care for nothing except for power, and who care for no one except themselves. I wonder how long before the mob realises that their so-called 'heroes' don't care about them either.

Meanwhile all they've succeeded in doing is divide people with hate. Lovely.

*26 March 2015*

# Battling Islamic State Influence

A bright spark in our Cabinet recently said that women joined IS because they were lonely. Actually women join all sorts of things if they are lonely – gyms, clubs, mosques and churches amongst others that are usually within their own vicinity. It doesn't explain however why there are a lot more men joining IS than women. Could they be even lonelier?

JAKIM has declared that they will now go on an all-out war against IS' influence. Of course this is a good thing and should be supported. But for any outside observer, it is too easy to see how JAKIM's good intentions will fail. The gap between such intentions and reality is simply too large.

JAKIM may think that issuing a fatwa against IS is the right move. In fact it makes hardly a dent. For one thing most people are not aware of any such fatwa. Secondly, such a fatwa is going to be ignored by IS recruiters because they obviously do not respect JAKIM's authority anyway. And their own fatwas, or opinions, on why it is a good thing to join IS, are far more seductive to certain impressionable people, male or female.

Saying that it is unIslamic to take up violence is certainly correct. Wanting to die a martyr's death, especially by suicide and killing others at the same time, is also forbidden in Islam. But it is not enough to stop at defining a terrorist merely as one who takes up arms and violence. We need to look more holistically at the issue of IS and who it directs its terror at.

For a start, who is IS fighting and inflicting violence on? Thus far they have terrorised just about anyone who disagrees with them, whether they are other Muslims especially Shias, other Sunnis who don't agree with them, non-Muslim civilian populations such as the Yezidis and Christians, foreign humanitarian workers, journalists and just about anybody who refuses to pledge allegiance to their cause.

So, the first thing we have to teach young people is to learn to accept that people have different views and beliefs. How do we do this when every day someone of a different opinion or faith is being persecuted just for disagreeing with the dominant faith or government, or for that matter, just being different? If at home we don't have any tolerance for people who disagree with us, how do we explain how IS treats differences in beliefs and views so violently? What is the difference between the way IS treats Shias in Syria for instance and the way we do here, except for the degree of violence?

This violence has forced huge numbers of ordinary Syrians to flee their homes. More than three million have fled to neighbouring countries increasing the burden on their already strained societies. Another six million people are internally displaced, meaning that they are forced to leave their homes to look for shelter from IS within their own country. But as IS expands the territory under its rule, these people have to constantly move to look for safety. Think of what this feels like, to be constantly afraid, to be unsure of how to feed their children, to have no access to healthcare, schools and jobs. IS has also done a good job of destroying infrastructure in Syria so that humanitarian aid cannot even reach these beleaguered civilians.

Why have we said nothing about these refugees? Why have we not extended help to them? And while we extend our sympathies to similar situations nearby, why then do we treat refugees in our own land so badly?

Then there's the way IS treats women. There is a horrific Human Rights Watch report based on interviews with women and girls who have escaped IS telling of the systematic abductions, rape, torture and murder of women in the IS-held territories. Most of the women were Yezidi, a small community in Syria, but some were also Muslim. Some of the horror stories involved girls as young as 12, raped by gangs of IS fighters. Many were sold as slaves, with IS claiming it is Islamic to do this to prisoners of war.

To counter IS at home, we thus need to teach our young to respect women and girls. We should have zero tolerance for violence against women and girls, regardless of what they wear, say or do. How do we do this when JAKIM is silent when women are threatened with rape for giving a different opinion on issues? Why are women constantly attacked just for speaking up?

This is why JAKIM's 'war' against IS will fail. As the Malay saying goes, 'cakap tak serupa bikin' or 'not walking the talk'. But there is another word for this: hypocrisy.

*23 April 2015*

# Equality for Women Still a Long Way Off

Do we women not matter at all? Are we only valuable around election time? Is the fact that we can vote the only indicator of our equality?

Women's groups were in shock last week when at a National Women's Day celebration, the minister for women, family and community development blithely stated that Malaysia had no need for a women's rights movement because we were given equality from the start. Now I understand that the remarks were off-the-cuff but it begs the question of how unimportant are Malaysian women viewed that they didn't merit a carefully prepared speech?

Some people can do off-the-cuff and some people can't. But the trouble is that when the speaker attempts to speak 'from the heart' as it were, what he says can betray his real attitudes. For one thing, nobody should speak off the cuff unless they know the subject well. And unfortunately our man didn't.

To say that we are better off than developed countries because we got the vote from the beginning is to skim the surface of history. Yes, developed countries did not give the vote to women 'from the beginning'. But they are also older countries, established during eras when archaic attitudes about women prevailed. When we gained independence, of course we had to give women the vote because by then attitudes towards women had changed.

But what is more important is what has happened since then. Switzerland did not give women the vote until the 1970s. But today they have had not only a woman president but half of their Cabinet are women. We on the other hand did not even appoint our first woman minister until a full 12 years after independence, despite the efforts that women put in during the independence struggle. What's more we only amended our Federal Constitution to prohibit gender-based discrimination as late as 2001, an act that even now is not fully implemented because a judge ruled that it does not apply to the private sector.

Gender-based violence is also a discrimination issue because it is women who tend to suffer more. If we had all our rights in 1957, why then did we need to fight for a Domestic Violence Act, a law that took six years to be passed by Parliament and a further two years before it could be gazetted? Why did we need a Law Reform (Marriage and Divorce) Act in 1976 if women did not think their situation was unfair? Why did we need the Guardianship of Infants (Amendment) Act in 1999 so that finally women could be recognised as guardians to their own children?

None of these changes that benefited women happened on their own. A recent study by two American academics showed that, far more than women politicians, women's groups are crucial in pushing for laws that benefit women. Similarly, Malaysian women's groups fought hard to gain these rights. They wrote memoranda, attended meetings, marched and protested. In the end they won some of the battles they fought.

Does this mean that we are now completely equal substantively to male citizens of this country? Of course not! Yes, we may be able to go to any golf club we want (although there are still bars in clubs we are prohibited from entering) but we might get sexually harassed there and we cannot complain, just as we can't if we face the same problem at work. We are expected to work outside the home, and indeed often have no other choice, but we are still expected to cook, clean and care. This double burden can be deeply stressful especially if we have no support. The government has called for crèches at workplaces, but they seem to have no will to enforce that in the private sector nor make them give longer maternity leave.

But we are proud that companies are now being compelled to include women on their Boards. All well and good but the numbers of women being trained to do so are nowhere near the 30% Government-mandated requirement. So, are we just meant to be tokens?

What is not mentioned is that when we signed up to the Convention for the Elimination of Discrimination Against Women (CEDAW) we said we would allocate women 30% of the positions in all decision-making positions. This means more than Boards; this includes political positions. So if we comply, we need to have nine women in the current Cabinet instead of the dismal two we used to have. What's more, in the coming elections, 30% of all candidates should also be women.

To say that we already have equality is to deny the very many reports on the status of women in this country that clearly state that we do not. Normally I'd blame whoever wrote the speech for such neglect of facts.

But when it's off the cuff, who do I blame?

*11 October 2012*

# Everything Is Not OK

World AIDS Day just went by with all the usual newspaper features on the current statistics in our country and the problems limiting our ability to contain the epidemic. Chief among these is stigma and discrimination, the perpetuation of myths and falsehoods about both the disease and the people who live with it, causing fear, secrecy and, sometimes, outright violations of the human rights of HIV-positive people and those around them.

It seems ironic to me that while World AIDS Day features in the papers aim to enlighten the public about HIV/AIDS, at the very same time, a group of people gathered to triumphantly tout their ignorance, their prejudice and their hate. Blaming all the ills of society on those most marginalised and vulnerable, they hooted and cawed their fears and directed their disgust towards a group they cannot clearly identify. Yet they claim that society may only be saved if we put the different and defenceless into camps, much like the people of Gaza are put into a large prison camp, to be punished for their 'mistake' of trying to choose their own destiny.

There is nothing more fascinating than watching a group so devoted to displaying such wilful hate. Some even called themselves God's chosen ones, a familiar phrase to those of us who follow Zionist politics. The implications of such a claim is obvious; if God has chosen some people to lead us, why the need for elections when voters would make the likely mistake of choosing the wrong ones? Why not just abandon elections and let God choose? Where have we heard this before? Is this theocracy-lite, without the turbans and beards?

So retrograde was the discussion at this assembly that it felt like a 1950s movie. Once again, we were told, by a woman no less, that we already have gender equality in this country and therefore there is no need for any women's rights activists. Coming from someone who has done very little to advance women's rights in this country, this can only be expected. After all, while demanding 30% of the seats for women in the next general elections, the same person had to ask a man to represent them to get permission for such allocations. Why ask yourself when you can ask a man to do it for you? Now that's 1950s activism, none of this feminism business!

I must say it was a sublime moment: the leader of a woman's movement triumphantly stating that there are no issues for women to fight for because everything is OK. Tell that to the many single mothers fighting for their rights in our courts, the many women who remain legally married but in reality have no spouses, the women who lose their property when their husbands die, the many women black and blue from beatings at the hands of their dearly beloveds every day. Tell that to our young women who after graduating find that some jobs are cut off from them because of their gender, or those who find jobs and then have to endure a workplace that is uncomfortable and subtly hostile through crass comments and even physical affronts. Or the many women bypassed for promotion by less-qualified men.

Like the targeting of minority and marginalised groups, this trumpeting of 'non-activism' is only a distraction from the pressing problems of the day. The word 'corruption' was barely heard at all, unless it referred to sexual mores as those are the only ones that can be corrupted. 'Ethics' was not in anyone's vocabulary, much less 'justice'. So insular was the talk that I don't even recall the words 'Gaza' or 'Rohingyas', even while thousands of our fellow brethren are suffering.

The trouble with insularity is that it ignores one simple fact: the world is watching. With smartphones, broadband and social media, what is said within any gathering is transmitted outside and all round the world in a second. Playing to the gallery may be a valid strategy within the confines of an exclusive group but with technology, there are now many different galleries all watching at the same time. I hope some people within the group had the decency to at least cringe at the more outrageous pronouncements.

If this is the pre-election rah-rah session, it truly baffles me how it would work. Those of us outside pay attention to get some idea of what we can hope for when we cast our votes in the next few months. But I'm probably not alone in finding little to hold on to except for a group that looks like it's under siege and is blaming everyone but itself for its own failures.

The rest of us, meanwhile, are already ticking our voting ballots.

*6 December 2012*

## Stop Violence Against Women

2012 ended on a mixed note. On the bright side, despite people believing in the Mayans' alleged predictions, the world did not end. On the other hand, the end of the year saw a most gruesome crime being committed that ended with the death of a young girl.

Regardless that it happened in India, the case of the young medical student gang-raped and beaten so viciously resonated with many of us here, especially with women. Facebook and Twitter were filled with many articles and comments about it. There were those who recoiled at the horror of it; there were also those who savoured the juicy details. Debates ensued as to why it happened. Many believe that this was the work of perverts.

In many ways they are right. But perverts work in certain circumstances. For one thing they don't work where they are unlikely to be successful. A late-night bus where it would be easy to intimidate the victim is just one. Another is if the potential victim is a young woman who is physically less able to fight back.

To say that such rapists are primarily motivated by lust is to introduce feelings that are not there, or to equate lust always with violence. This was a gang rape. How does each individual perpetrator have exactly the same 'feelings' towards the victim? Doesn't the fact that they are in a group embolden them more, makes them feel more powerful? Isn't this yet another bit of proof that rape, and violence against women in general, is nothing to do with sex or lust but about power? Separate each individual of the gang and see if they are as brave.

Neither is it a crime that's only found in other 'less-developed' countries. Let's not forget that we have had similar cases, with names like Noor Shuzaily, Canny Ong and Nurin Jazlin. These were no less horrible cases and in the case of little Nurin, still unsolved. Who knows how many more of these there are? Yet do we do much soul-searching, let alone go out and hold protests and candlelight vigils as they have done in India? In India, things might finally change for women there. In Malaysia, nothing much has.

We look in horrified derision at the United States with its absurd gun laws and where there is no will to do anything about a society where kids can have access to guns and easily kill so many others, as just happened in Newtown. We blame the movies for some of it. Yet we don't apply the same insight to our own media. No, we don't promote guns in our movies but we do promote a certain way of treating women, one where it is deemed alright for a woman to be raped and then 'redeem' herself by marrying her rapist. Once again the onus, burden and shame is on the woman victim and not the perpetrator. We also have movies where rape is seen as justified punishment for women who gossip, where the perpetrator of the crime is let off. So we cut out scenes of kissing but think it's okay for these sorts of messages to be kept.

These are just a few of the ways in which women are put in their 'place' every day. Today the most popular local novels emphasise that a good woman is one who obeys her man, regardless of how unjust he may be to her. Our preachers instil in our men that, even if they earn less and take no responsibility for their families, they are superior to women. Women do everything to keep their families together and put food on the table, and still are told that they are a degree less than men.

No wonder then on social media, rape is still blamed on women and mostly on how they dress and behave. How that explains what happened to Noor Shuzaily who had her hair neatly covered and was on her way to work in the morning, is a mystery. Should she not have worked outside the home at all?

In 2013, I truly hope that Malaysians will finally take violence against women seriously. There is not a single woman who has not felt intimidated and unsafe when she is out alone, in the company of strangers or having to walk on the streets. There is not a mother who doesn't fear for her daughters every time they go out. Don't we all have daughters who are medical students just weeks away from getting married too, just like the girl in New Delhi?

It all starts at the top. My vote will go to whichever government will treat women with respect and stop violence against women.

Happy New Year!

*3 January 2013*

# The Way To Defend Women's Rights

On International Women's Day this year, some Afghan men did an extraordinary thing. They paraded in Kabul wearing the burqa to draw attention to the issue of women's rights in their country, or rather the lack of women's rights.

In most countries, events on International Women's Day are mostly by women and for women. Rarely do men ever do something to show that they too are concerned about the violation of women's rights.

When men do, they are often ham-fisted about it. Last year I was on a panel with two other prominent women talking about issues affecting women at work when an earnest young man stood up to ask how a wife can support her husband in his work. This was a fine example of male tone-deafness and the inability to understand the milieu he was in and therefore the clanging awkwardness of that question. I have also been at women's forums where men get up to declare how much they love women and manage to sound condescending and creepy at the same time. We don't want you to just love us, we also want you to respect us as equals.

Men can also be blindsided by the dazzle of a few women. When there is an outstanding woman whom men respect, they tend to think that these women are exceptions. To them, it is not normal for women to be so good at what they think of as men's jobs, so these women are not the rule but the exceptions that prove it. I have seen men become totally dumbfounded when asked to name expert women in a particular field apart from the one they see in the papers all the time. They assume that no other ones exist. A little research, with the assistance of their female assistants, would have unearthed many.

In some cases, men think they are doing women a favour by 'defending' them in very masculine ways. In India, a mob attacked a jail where a suspected rapist was being held, stripped him naked and then beat him to death. What difference does this actually make to the female victim, who would still be shunned by society, and to other women who still face the same dangers every day? This murderous act was done more to avenge the honour of the men to whom the woman 'belonged', rather than in defence of the woman herself.

And interestingly enough, when I posted an article about the Delhi rapist blaming his victim for her own death, among the many violent reactions from men was one calling him a derogatory female epithet. The highest insult to a man is to call him a woman because we are still lesser beings.

In our own country, we can hardly find any man who would stand up publicly in support of women's rights. Instead we have men who can find a myriad of justifications why women get raped, beaten, summarily divorced, denied positions of leadership and so on. When women call them out on it, they retreat and then deny what they said or wrote. But how many men, from the same community, told him off? Did their silence mean they agreed with him?

There are many men out there who do not believe that women deserve to have such horrific treatment meted out on them. These men are well aware that women gave birth to them and cared for them until adulthood and that they have sisters and wives on whom they would never wish such violence.

But at the same time they are cowed by the culture of machoness where to talk about women's rights is to be a traitor to their sex. Where sometimes even their own sexuality can become suspect, just because they defend women. That such a culture can be also oppressive to them is something they are oblivious to. Why should any man be vilified just for being a decent human being?

When we teach young boys that violence towards those they perceive as weaker than them is alright, then we should also prepare them to live in a world where there will be nothing except violence all the time. They will have to spend their time always having to fight either someone weaker or someone stronger than them. Why would we want to subject our sons to this? Won't they ever get sick of it?

Gender inequality may seem like fair sport to some but studies have proven that it does nothing except drag a whole society down to its most primitive levels. Gender equality, exemplified by less violence against women, benefits both sexes and allows a country to progress.

Perhaps we should ask the misogynists whether what they really want is a society with only men?

*12 March 2015*

# Uniformity Is Not Unity

I had occasion to fly on three very bumpy flights recently and had a macabre thought: even though everyone on the flight was a stranger to me, my destiny then was tied to theirs. If we arrived safely at our destination, our shared destiny was to survive. If not, then…well, I would not be here writing this.

It got me thinking that, however briefly, all the passengers on the flight, and on any flight, are united by this shared destiny. Whatever happens will happen almost equally to every single one. If an accident happens, different people may have different fates but none of them can actually avoid going through the accident and none of them can be privileged enough to ensure a better outcome.

For instance, no one on the plane can insist on a different fate because they are of an elite class or race or religion. Just because you're seated in first class doesn't mean that you will be spared any injury in the event of a crash. I've never heard of anyone escaping unscathed just because they belong to any particular faith.

So basically, all passengers on the plane, regardless of who they are, where they are from or what they believe in, are united by their shared fate.

Our country is like that plane too. All of us are on the same plane and our destiny is a shared one. Some of us may be sitting in the front of the plane and most of us will be at the back. But we're all hopefully going to the same place. If the flight gets bumpy, all of us will feel it. If it is smooth, we can all take a snooze.

The concept of unity espoused by some people however puzzles me. First, they think that all the people on that plane should be entirely the same. I suppose you can charter a plane to take you somewhere but if something happens to that plane, it leaves behind lots of people who aren't the same as you.

Secondly, if everyone is the same on that plane, what could possibly be new and different to talk about on the flight? One journey would be all you would need and then you basically remove any need for any more flights ever again. Whereas if you had lots of different people onboard, then there would always be something to talk about – where to go, how to get there, what to do once you're there – so you give yourselves many opportunities to fly to all sorts of exciting destinations.

Some people seem to mistake uniformity for unity. Everyone would not only look the same but also think and act the same. I don't know of any country where everyone is forced to be the same that also develops in a forward-looking way. North Korea would be the best example. Other countries like Japan or South Korea may look homogenous but in fact they are not. That's why they can be very creative. They also have no qualms about borrowing ideas from other countries and improving on them in their own way. Their people, however, do understand that they're all on that same plane together.

But over here, some people's idea of unity is for half the country to come together and the other half to dumbly sit back and wait for scraps. Or to belabour that airplane analogy, half the plane is first class while the rest are in cattle class. But I read somewhere that the front of the plane isn't necessarily the safest place to be if anything should happen.

What's more if you have an unskilled pilot, or one who is asleep in the cockpit, then everyone's fate depends on what he does or doesn't do. Even if the most advanced jets today can virtually fly themselves, they still need human brains and hands to land them safely. So the passengers can argue all they want but none of them will be able to fly that aircraft.

So we need to be clear about what unity means, and that the reason we need to have unity is because we have diversity. That diversity is a given and we can't wish it away no matter how much we want to. But diversity is actually an asset because it is in managing our differences that we learn how to negotiate, compromise and respect one another. No innovation ever came out of uniformity.

We therefore have a choice. Get onboard the flight together and accept our common destiny. Or fight over where you're going to sit and who's going to get the best food.

Buckle your seat belts please!

*28 February 2014*

# Our Blood Is All The Same Red Colour

In the past few days, the shock of the disappearance of MH370 has been overwhelming. Undoubtedly the families have suffered the greatest shock of all, especially when not even the tiniest explanation (at the time of writing) is forthcoming. Hopes are built up and then dashed. Theories are put forth but none are yet proven. Everyone seems to have an opinion regardless of whether they know anything about jet planes or aeronautics. And let's not forget those who take the opportunity to place blame on the most outlandish reasons. A bit like when some blamed the Indian Ocean tsunami on people partying on beaches.

The wiser among us keep our own counsel and instead turn our efforts to offering words of comfort to those who are missing their families. This also includes colleagues of the flight crew who have known them a long time and worked alongside them. So many people are grieving over this incident, and that's only on this side. We don't even know what's truly happening among the families of the Chinese passengers, and all the other nationalities involved and what support they might need. (And it occurred to me that our children are also aware of what happened and need some gentle explanations.)

But if anything exemplifies how small a country we are, it is the incredible fact that although there were only 38 Malaysians on MH370, so many people know them either first-hand or second-hand. I read my Facebook timeline and it was incredible how many people either knew the passengers or crew directly or knew their relatives or someone else close to them. A colleague reported that the wife of one of the cabin crew is her daughter's kindergarten teacher. Seems so random but yet not.

Perhaps this is why Malaysians are sharing this shock and grief so keenly. It's been hard to read the many sad posts and tweets from family members without imagining that it could have happened to any of us. As a result, Malaysians have turned to their own talents to express both their grief and support. So many beautiful images inviting people to pray for MH370 have been created and shared by people on social media. They are invitations to us all to do something together.

Many prayer events of different faiths have been organised for people to pray for the safe return of the plane, crew and passengers. Several religious groups have gone to KLIA to provide spiritual support to the families. I think in times like these, nobody is going to be particular about religious territoriality.

A group of citizens calling themselves Malaysians for Malaysia, that has been promoting peace and unity, and which I'm very proud to be part of, decided on a simple initiative called Walls of Hope. We approached various shopping malls around the Klang Valley to ask if they could put up something where the public can put up messages of hope and support for the families of MH370. Unsurprisingly the malls agreed almost immediately and got their art departments to design something and put them up at a prominent position on their premises. Pavilion KL was the first to put up theirs and within an hour, 1000 people had put messages up. Fahrenheit 88 followed soon after and they too found the public responding enthusiastically. At this time of writing, several other malls are organising themselves to do the same and we hope others around the country will do so too. These walls or trees of hope provide an outlet for Malaysians and foreigners to express their grief but also their hopes and wishes for those on board the flight as well as the families. Just reading so many heartfelt messages is a moving experience.

But if anything exemplifies how Malaysians are a compassionate and caring people, it is the poem written by a woman called Pnut Syafinaz which I had the privilege of reading out on TV.

To quote from it, in reference to the grieving families of the passengers on MH370,

*Jiwa kami dan jiwa mereka tidak sama,*
*Kami sedih tetapi tidak akan ada yang lebih sedih dari mereka,*
*Mereka dan kami mungkin bukan sebangsa, seagama,*
*tetapi darah kami sama merah pekat warnanya*

Our souls and their souls are not the same,
We are sad but can't be as sad as they,
They and us may not be the same race or religion,
But our blood is all the same red colour.

And that's the crux of the matter. Ultimately, in times like these, it really doesn't matter who anyone is, where they came from or what they believed in. Their families and friends all suffer pain just the same.

Let's continue to pray for MH370.

*14 March 2014*

# A Watershed Moment

The news we had been dreading came last night. MH370 is gone. The grief of the families is unbearable. The pain is no less so for the very many of us who have followed the story every step of the way, and who have tried to provide hope and support to the families either directly or indirectly through our prayers. I extend my deepest condolences to all the mothers, fathers, children, other relatives, friends and colleagues of those who were lost. May the souls of the passengers and crew of MH370 rest in peace.

The writer Tash Aw, in an op-ed for the *New York Times*, described this incident as a watershed moment for Malaysia. While not all our reasons synchronise, I do agree that MH370 has thrown up a huge mirror upon which we can see much that is wrong with us, as well as some that is right. I think this moment changed some things here in Malaysia and hopefully will also lead to some more changes.

The initial handling of the crisis was bumbling and inept but we can see that this changed very quickly. An airline disaster cannot be confined to just domestic news. By its nature, it is instantly international news and therefore the world's focus is immediately on us. There could not be a worse way to get our name known.

But we have a crisis and we need to handle it in the full glare of international media. This necessitates a totally different way of working than our officials are used to. For one thing it throws up the dire need for our officials to be able to speak English clearly and precisely and to not get defensive when faced with tougher questions than they are used to. For another it also shows up the quality of our media compared to the foreign media (except for that French reporter). Couldn't the reporter from the Islamic TV channel have looked at a map first before asking the minister if there was any city nearer to the search site in the southern Indian Ocean than Perth? Why do vernacular media send reporters who do not speak English and then complain that they did not understand what was said? Is this our flip-flop education policy on English coming to roost?

Coming to roost also is a certain complacency that has resulted in what one overseas academic has observed (before this happened) to be a 'reduction in capacity' among Malaysian officials. It is a lowering of standards which leads to a slowness in grasping a situation and then responding which, in this case, may have led to fatal results. It is the same with everything here; we don't react until something bad happens. Then we make a lot of noise about changing systems but don't actually implement them. We can never be considered serious about this complacency if we never hold anyone responsible for mistakes and missteps.

This points also to a lack of empathy on the part of some people for the suffering of those closest to the tragedy. Although thousands of Malaysians have shown their sympathy and kindness to the families by writing their messages on the Walls of Hope around the country, some saw fit by defacing them by writing unrelated slogans. Their issue may well have its merits but this act displays a lack of sensitivity to the families in terrible pain right now. Not a great way to win over people to your cause.

Disgusting is the only word for the insensitive tweet sent to the daughter of one of the MH370 cabin crew harshly telling her to accept the loss of her father. Many have done little more than condemn every single action done by MAS almost as if this tragedy is something it welcomed. I've had many complaints about MAS before but who would want to be in their shoes right now and say they can do a better job at handling this? They are also a bereaved party after all.

Certainly there is no lack of opportunists taking advantage of MH370 for their own ends. That would include some of the foreign media who seem intent on painting our government as completely inept. Certainly they are deficient in many aspects but I don't think they were wrong to be cautious with information. One reporter actually saw fit to ask the MAS chairman if they had been heartless. Did they expect an affirmative answer?

For now there is not a lot we laypersons can do other than to pray and hope that MH370 will reveal itself soon and that its discovery will provide us with some answers. Then we would know how to move on to the next phase of this watershed moment.

That next phase has to involve much introspection and self-critical analysis. We need to reflect very deeply on what we want for our country now that this incident has reminded us that we are part of the world, and not some isolated, opaque, inward-looking nation.

*28 March 2014*

# Improving Education

A recent headline claimed that Malaysia's education system is fast becoming the world's best. I really had to blink several times because it seemed as far-fetched a claim as Malaysian women now being equal to our men. Further down in the article it said that we still had a long way to go before we could 'justly' the claim that we are at par with the world's best.

Once again, we are handed a confusing statement. Are we improving or are we not? According to our Government Transformation Plan report, 'The rate of improvement of the system in the last 15 years is among the fastest in the world'. But that actually says very little because it can mean that while 15 people can now read when previously there were ten, it still means there are only 15 literate people.

I really wish newspapers would ask tougher questions of pronouncements like these. One of the GTP targets is to get 92% enrolment in pre-schools. For a long time, we have been proud of our literacy rates. But it turns out we measure our literacy rates through school enrolment rates, which any schoolchild will tell you is not the same thing. That is, just because you went to school doesn't mean you're literate. Indeed just because you pass our school exams, it doesn't mean you're literate either, as any frustrated employer can tell you. So achieving high enrolment should be only part of the goal, the rest is about giving our children quality education.

Undoubtedly there are supposed to be four key GTP initiatives to improve the quality of education but this does not necessarily translate into a 'fast-improving' education system. Our problems are so numerous yet the reforms needed in our education system are moving at a glacial pace, compared with the world our kids will grow up in.

I also have a problem with the stated target of reducing the rural–urban achievement gap by 25%. What is the gap in the first place? If it is huge, is reducing it by 25% enough? When will this be achieved? In another study a few years ago, urban parents who cannot afford to care for their children in the cities are sending them to their home villages to be cared for by their grandparents. Undoubtedly the schooling that these kids will get will be inferior to what is available in the city, not to mention other disadvantages they will have including the lack of civic amenities in the rural areas. What's more, the family background they will be in may not be as conducive to high achievement as if they stayed with their own parents, who are in all likelihood better educated than the grandparents. Are these issues considered in the Education blueprint? What would be the psychological cost of separating children from their parents for most of their impressionable years?

While a good educational foundation is good for our children, we should also not neglect the other end of the educational scale, tertiary education. Assuming our children survive their early education to get to tertiary education, what happens there? As it is, employers are complaining about the quality of the graduates we bring out. What are we doing about this end?

And here's a question: if our students coming out of public

universities are not meeting employable standards, how is it that we are going all out to market our universities to foreign students? What will they get out of it? It makes me wonder why any foreign student would want to come here and study because if the quality of our local graduates are not up to par, then they cannot be much better off.

But yet in our public universities, there are thousands upon thousands of foreign students here. How do we select them? Are we selecting the best and the brightest, or just anyone who can pay the fees? What exactly is our reason for opening up our very low-ranking universities to foreign students?

A neighbour of ours has made it their policy to give scholarships to the best and the brightest from the countries around them. In this way they not only attract the best brains to study there but eventually these brains don't want to go home. Even if they do, like all foreign students who study overseas, they will retain friendly ties with the country of their alma mater, useful for both parties for the future.

Our policy however is not to invest in brains, whether it's ours or other people's. As long as foreign students pay to put their warm bodies behind our desks, we don't care what they have to offer. And then feign surprise when some of them get up to some very troublesome activities.

*30 March 2013*

# Teach for Malaysia

Occasionally one should have experiences that keep one grounded in reality. I had one such opportunity recently when I participated in Teach for Malaysia Week. Teach for Malaysia is an organisation that places young future leaders, who have had the benefit of an excellent education, as teachers in schools in less affluent areas around Malaysia. These teachers spend two years helping to learn about and address inequities in our education system in order to change the lives of less privileged kids.

Every year various public figures from all walks of life are invited to go to one of the TFM schools and teach a class. The idea is not only to allow the kids the opportunity to interact with people with wide experience in different fields but also for the TFMW participants to both support the TFM teachers and also get an idea, however brief, of what our public schools are like today.

I was assigned to a secondary school with about 1200 students in small-town Perak. My Fourth Form class had 25 students who my co-teacher had already told me are a lively bunch. We are free to decide what we want to talk to them about and I chose travel as an entry point to talk about many different subjects.

The first thing I noticed was that the girls in the class outnumbered the boys by two to one. Was this an indication that boys tend to drop out after Form Three? And will do so even more in later schooling years, hence the reason why female undergrads outstrip male undergrads in our universities? What then do our boys do if they don't continue their education? Should we not find out why this is happening?

Secondly, apart from four students, the class was almost entirely mono-ethnic. And the four were all from the smallest of our three main ethnic groups. Our second-largest group was wholly absent from the class and, it seemed to me, from the entire school. Did this mean that there are absolutely no Chinese families in the area, or that they all go to some other school? In which case, what happens to kids who grow up with absolutely no interactions with major Malaysian communities during their school years?

It could be that part of the answer is to ensure that our public schools meet certain academic standards. The school I went to ranks somewhere over 1000 out of 2000 schools in the country. It's not for want of dedicated teachers. The principal of the school I went to talked about how he's trying to improve the results from the students but it's been a difficult, thankless job. Although so many studies show that when parents are involved in their children's schooling, kids do much better, the principal has been hard-pressed to encourage more parent involvement. He's tried organising PTA meetings at days and times most suited to parents' schedules, yet only 100 parents turn up out of the possible 1000. How do we get busy parents more involved and included in their children's schooling?

Despite this, I had an enjoyable time with my class. They were inquisitive and not shy about asking questions. They shouted answers to my questions even though they were guessing more than knowing the answers. The girls noticeably participated more than the boys. My co-teacher, the TFM 'Fellow', has been able to create a conducive learning atmosphere in just three months. However the ethnic minority behaved like a minority; they were too quiet. Perhaps we should not allow them to sit together, apart from the rest of the class.

What I tried to impart to them was that they are part of this big world that we share with so many other people. Travel is important because it enables us to get to know different people and cultures, and that no one people or culture is superior to another. While actual travel may be out of their reach at the moment, travelling via books is not, so I tried to encourage them to read as much as possible.

My short stint as a teacher gave me a real appreciation of what schools are like outside the relative affluence of the Klang Valley. As the principal told me, there is a problem of confidence both among the students and among teachers especially if they feel they are stuck in the lowest ranks of schools. Perhaps part of the solution is to make teaching a more creative endeavour than it currently is.

And perhaps we need politicians to also do stints in schools and face the questions the kids ask themselves. It might bring them down to earth with a crash.

*13 April 2013*

# Comparative Religion from the Earliest Years

For three consecutive years I've been invited to speak to a group of Norwegian students visiting Malaysia about the work that my colleagues and I do on Muslim women's rights. These students are learning about different faiths in order to be better able to teach comparative religions back home in Norway. Instead of merely learning about all these religions in theory, every year their university organises a trip for them to visit various Southeast Asian countries in order to observe first-hand how these religions are lived and practised.

In Norway, every child learns about comparative religions from the age of six with the idea that they will grow up understanding the diversity of faiths and beliefs in their society and the world today, and to respect all the faiths equally. The books they use are vetted and approved by the respective religious authorities, so, for example, the Norwegian Islamic authorities approve the books on Islam.

The students who came to listen to me will eventually become the teachers of those Norwegian schoolkids. Lest anyone think they only get to listen to 'liberals' like me, they also meet and talk to all sorts of people with knowledge on the religious landscape in our country, including in our universities. This is to ensure that they get a balanced picture of things in Malaysia.

I was really impressed by this approach by the Norwegian government to address potential issues in a rapidly diversifying society. Obviously one of the ways to avoid conflict in society is by ensuring that everybody understands each other. Including comparative religions in their school curriculum from the earliest years means that young children will become used to religious and cultural diversity naturally and hopefully will grow to become adults who are respectful of religions other than their own. In a study comparing the English and Norwegian comparative religious curriculums and how schoolchildren reacted to them, most of the students viewed the classes positively, with one student saying, 'It is important to understand religions in order to understand humans, sort of improving our social intelligence a little.'

It is interesting that Norway, with a population of under six million people, 82% of whom are Lutheran Christian, are so concerned about the possible conflict that ethnic and religious diversity might cause that, from 1997, they decided to educate people on religions other than their own. Undoubtedly their concern was well-founded when in 2011 Anders Brevik, a self-confessed fascist and hater of multiculturalism, murdered 77 people blaming them for allowing immigrants into the country. Norway, too, is home to many right-wing groups claiming white supremacy and that Muslims are taking over Norway, despite being all of 3.6% of the population. Perhaps it is in the nature of supremacist groups everywhere to make up stories about threats to their people without the need for supporting evidence.

Still the policy of educating children about religions other than their own is a step in the right direction. And bringing students to countries where those other religions are the faith of the majority helps to humanise those faiths, and prevents the stereotyping that extremists like to do.

It's too bad that if anyone were to raise the issue of including comparative religions lessons in our schools, our own religious supremacists will undoubtedly go ballistic, claiming that this was a plot by a majority Muslim government to Christianise their people, as ironic as that may sound. Obviously supremacists all work from the same manual. There is no evidence that learning about different religions in school, with each (including atheism by the way) given equal weight, has led to the conversion of anyone to another religion. It does however, based on my experience with these Norwegian students, lead to far more intelligent questions than from those of my own faith.

Meanwhile few people here in Malaysia are coming up with any bright ideas on how to reduce the polarisation that everyone acknowledges is a growing problem in our society. The best that anyone can come up with is putting everyone in the same school, which would be a good solution if the standard of education in those schools were higher (as measured globally) and that everyone was taught to respect differences. But the way they are now, even many Muslims do not want to send their children there if they can afford it.

Our children live in a multireligious society in which they won't be able to avoid noticing that different people worship differently. If they ask questions of adults around them, do we take our inability to answer as a personal affront or as an opportunity to learn? The former is the arrogant way, while the latter is more humble.

Which should we choose if we genuinely want peace and harmony?

*29 January 2015*

# It All Boils Down to Education

In the end it all boils down to the same thing: education.

I was reading an international newspaper and two articles struck me because of their similarities. One was a story about the French minister of education, Najat Vallaud-Belkacem. Madame Vallaud-Belkacem is the first woman to be made minister of education in France. More remarkably, she is both a Moroccan immigrant and Muslim.

Madame Vallaud-Belkacem has been put in charge of educating young French people about the dangers of radicalism, the type of so-called religious fervour that led to the *Charlie Hebdo* shootings. She believes that schools have a big role to play in this. And indeed she is living proof.

The minister was born in Morocco but went to France with her mother and older sister to join her construction-worker father. There, her five younger siblings were born and the entire family lived in poverty in a small northern city. Madame Vallaud-Belkacem credits the French education system with giving her the opportunities she has had, and which allowed her to enter politics and eventually be where she is now.

But she also understands that it is because of the poor education that most immigrant youth, especially Muslim youth, receive that drive them to become radicalised and to want to take up arms against their perceived enemies, both at home in France and abroad. These youth are poorly educated because of discrimination. At the same time, that poor education sets them up for even more discrimination, especially in the job market. This creates frustration and anger and makes them vulnerable to the sort of easy answers that radical preachers may provide.

The other story was about Nigeria where stereotypes about the Muslim north and the Christian south abound. The author of the article, Adaobi Tricia Nwaubani, a Christian, recalled that when she was growing up, there were special boarding schools that were set up to help the different Nigerian communities understand one another. These schools offered a high quality education and had quotas for the different communities so that they had a diverse mix of students.

However there was a persistent problem of poor education in the north of the country. The quota system ensured that many northerners got jobs but often without the same level of education as the southerners. That same low quality education meant that the northerners also did not value education for their own people, leading to a constant downward spiral of frustration due to the lack of opportunities despite the richness of resources in the region. This created conflict with southerners who were more educated and thus could avail themselves of better opportunities.

Needless to say, the north is also the home of Boko Haram, a violent group that has a particular distaste for education, particularly Western-style education. The exploits of Boko Haram are now well-known and suffice to say that only uneducated people would think nothing of sending out eight-year old girls as suicide bombers.

The point of these two stories is clear: the root of all sorts of societal problems, including religious radicalism and violence, is education. More specifically, the type of education we provide our children will predict what they will do in the future. Poor quality education, that does not prepare our children for a competitive global market, will be the root of all sorts of trouble, including the kind where 14-year old girls think it's exciting to go to Syria to marry a gun-toting stranger she met on Facebook.

We are seeing now the beginnings of the true results of our messed-up education system. Our young people are unable to think beyond what is immediate and exciting. They actually believe that you can get to heaven by killing people for reasons they are unable to articulate. These are not illiterate people but are certainly not educated in the broadest sense of the word.

On social media we find many many people who are unable to reason things out, nor able to accept different points of view. They are absolutely certain they are right, mostly because people they see as authoritative have convinced them that authority is always correct, even when those in authority tell them to do things that are patently wrong, such as to discriminate against or kill those different from them. Not all human beings are equal, is a mantra they are hearing every day.

'All men are not equal', by the way, was the chilling ideology I happened to read at the site of the former headquarters of the SS, the Nazi stormtroopers, in Berlin recently. And the propaganda the SS used had an uneasy familiarity to it.

And what is propaganda after all but another form of public education?

*26 February 2015*

# Disturbing Tales from Learning Hubs

Two stories this past week made me despair about our education system, indeed our entire educational environment.

One was the story about one of our local universities having come up with an 'anti-hysteria' kit costing more than 8000 ringgit. I really would not know where to put my face if ever asked by foreign friends about this. Without giving a single shred of evidence, nor any explanation about how it even works, a university lecturer, backed by his supervisors, proudly unveiled what he deemed a 'scientific' way of dealing with all sorts of supernatural beings which apparently cause hysteria mostly in boarding schools. Rarely have we seen the words 'scientific' and 'supernatural' in the same purportedly serious sentence.

But worse than the fact that time and money were wasted on such a ludicrous project were some of the reactions to it. Some comments criticised critics for being irreligious snobs, accusing them of only praising inventions made by (presumably unbelieving) Westerners while deriding local ones. What they fail to understand is that Western universities, and even many in the East, are not spending their resources researching ways to deal with goblins and ghosts, but are instead trying to find ways to cure diseases such as HIV and cancers or, like two young women from Columbia University, a way of helping victims of natural disasters with the help of a solar-powered LED light.

But worse than these ill-informed comments is the fact that the launch of the anti-hysteria kit was at the Ministry of Education building in Putrajaya. Does this mean that the MoE actually endorses this? If it does, then it truly illuminates what the officials in there think about education, that it is simply a conduit to feed our young with mumbo-jumbo, and while you're at it, make money as well.

Considering that all this hysteria only occurs in government boarding schools, mostly religious ones, and never at private secular ones, or at public universities, never private ones, could it be that the inventor of this kit believes that the market for it is actually the government? Imagine if the MoE purchased a kit for every single boarding school it runs, much like first aid kits or fire extinguishers. Someone would certainly make a pretty penny. Like everything else procured in this way, who cares if it works or not?

The other disturbing story is the one about an otherwise bright boy caught and jailed in London for downloading, making and distributing child pornography. Both the story and the reaction by Malaysians are puzzling me.

How does a very intelligent boy get into a prestigious university like Imperial College, and then totally blow his life away like this? What sort of background did he have that led him to this incredibly depraved crime? If he came from the same school system as all other Malaysian kids, one that apparently stressed religious and moral values, how could he have gone down this incredibly sick path?

Few people seemed to have noted that this boy was not just delving in any pornography; he was downloading and distributing child pornography. Do people even understand what that means? The Crimes Against Children Research Centre in the US defines child pornography as 'the visual depiction of sexually explicit conduct includes acts such as intercourse, bestiality and masturbation as well as lascivious exhibition of the genitals or pubic area'.

The London police said that the 30,000 images and videos they found on his computer and other devices were some of the worst they had ever seen. Most people seemed to have also missed one point: he was not only downloading images of children being sexually abused, he was making them. The CACRC reports that 'Most children exploited are pre-adolescent. Some children appear to have been subjected to physical as well as sexual violence.'

Do you think five years of jail is enough for such a person? Have any of our religious leaders condemned this terrible crime?

Yet his sponsors seem to think that he was only sentenced to nine months and would be home in about four weeks. I don't know on what basis they are disputing the British newspaper reports when one can simply go to the court and check what the sentence was. All they seem to be concerned about is recovering their scholarship money. But when he comes home, what is to be done with him? Oh I know, send him to the 'scientist' with the anti-hysteria kit. Surely it was just mischievous goblins that made him abuse young children.

There are even his 'supporters' online who insist that we must not shame him in public. These are the very same people who are quick to publicly shame anyone, especially women, who makes lifestyle choices they may not agree with. Yet this boy is a certifiable danger to our children. He needs rehabilitation, of the scientific psychological kind, not mumbo jumbo.

Both these stories are sad testimonies to the state of our education system. I'd like to think they are aberrations. But given the sympathetic response by both officials and some of the public and the inability to see what is wrong with these two cases, I think they are not.

*7 May 2015*

# Whipping Up a Fury

Some time last week one of our state religious departments proudly announced that it had subjected 24 women and 17 men to a whipping for the 'crime' of incest and sex outside of marriage. They even recommended that the next round should be done in public because the sight of the agonised faces of the victims is apparently sure to induce fear in anyone watching, thereby lessening these crimes.

Actually, if anyone has ever watched public spectacles such as canings and any sort of public humiliation of individuals, the last thing that happens is that the audience feels empathy with the victims. Instead they tend to take the side of the punisher and encourage them even more, partly in the belief that this makes them seem more righteous. Few ever put themselves in the shoes of the humiliated, believing that it will never happen to them.

So the logic that such a punishment will act as a deterrent is faulty, just as the death penalty has never deterred anyone from trafficking drugs in our country. Those who say that without these laws, things would have been worse have never been able to provide the evidence for it.

It's interesting that our morbid interest in public punishments only extends to women and only for sexual crimes. Why not for murder or drug trafficking, where the perpetrators are more likely to be men? Would that not deter men from such crimes?

More faulty is the logic behind punishing women for incest. As in statutory rape, incest is equally a problem of power dynamics, where one party, usually the woman, is unable to refuse sexual overtures from someone who has more power than her. In this case, the person is her father, uncle or brother. Often the abuse has been happening for years effecting all sorts of trauma for the victims. Why compound it by punishing her, and then multiplying it by wanting to do it in public? Why do we shake our heads in disgust at Western men who lock up their daughters in basements in order to rape them and yet feel nothing when the same happens to our girls?

In this case, the 'partners' in these crimes were also whipped. However, there were considerably less men punished than there were women, and the media chose to highlight only the women. Perhaps this is because they were keenly aware that our Federal Constitution forbids the whipping of women and therefore, despite the entreaties of our authorities, immediately sensationalised the case.

What sort of a country do we live in when, after 56 years of never whipping women, we now do so? How is this progress? How do we call ourselves moderate when we want to engage in public spectacles of such a barbaric nature?

If my 13-year old daughter reads that women are being caned for incest, what do I tell her? Don't commit incest so you won't be whipped? Does that make sense when it is unlikely to be her fault?

Our society has such an aversion to serious self-reflection that we fall back on the most medieval approaches to any issue even though none have been proven to work. Instead of the hard work that it takes to truly do prevention, instead of the care that should go into the protection of women and children from abuse, we choose the easy and lazy route. It must surely be the victims' fault and we must therefore punish them.

Then we wonder why, when we allow the true perpetrators of such crimes to get away, the issue keeps recurring. Does it occur to no one that if we have harsh, and unjust, punishments for victims, it will send the message that they can never hope to get justice for the suffering they have undergone? What would be the incentive then to report the abuse that is happening to them?

Unless of course our leaders do not think this abuse is serious or warrants much concern. How else do you explain the silence with which our political leaders have greeted this barbaric act by the state religious department? Apart from women's groups, no women politicians have said anything about this. Are the women who were whipped and their families not voters? Does winning allow impunity?

This shameful whipping episode illuminates the illness that besets our society today, where the fear of what others think overrides the fear of being unjust to another. Indeed, the injustice being perpetrated is not just against 24 women but all Malaysian women who now feel that the state is the last place to go for help.

*29 June 2013*

# A Mockery of Statutory Rape Law

There were two stories I read recently which were published side by side. One was about a 71-year-old man caught in a *khalwat* situation with a 14-year-old girl. Next to it was a story from India in which a 16-year-old boy was desperate to stop his parents from marrying off his 14-year-old sister but sadly was too late.

I was struck by one thing: neither of these stories included the words 'statutory rape'. Section 376 of the Malaysian Penal Code defines statutory rape as sexual intercourse with a girl under the age of 16 whether or not she has given consent. Discounting the second case because it is outside Malaysia, still why did no police go after the 71-year-old man for statutory rape? And why did the reporter not bring it up?

At a time when politicians and law enforcers keep harping about the citizenry always obeying the law, how come they get to ignore it? Two cases have made a mockery of our statutory rape law that carries a mandatory jail term of 20 years and mandatory whipping for each count upon conviction. One was when the court refused to jail Nor Afizal Azizan for raping a 13-year-old girl as 'taking into account that he is a national champion, the Court of Appeal ruled that it is not in the public interest as Noor Afizal has a promising future.' Good thing the South African court trying Oscar Pistorius isn't thinking that way because he certainly had a brighter future than Noor Afizal.

Then in the same month, the Penang Sessions Court released

Chuah Guan Jiu who had been convicted on two counts of raping his 12-year old girlfriend because 'the sexual act was consensual and that he is a school dropout'. The judge also took into account that this was Chuah's first offence, and that he was considering his future. Hopefully his future doesn't include continually raping his girlfriend for another four years until she reaches the age of consent.

When the law is clear on these crimes yet judges ignore them, then what is the public to make of it? The public loses its sense of what is lawful and what is not. Three years ago, a movie was made the premise of which was that a young woman was sold into prostitution by her own uncle, then bought by a rich man who repeatedly rapes her. Then in order that she not feel any more shame, she begs the man to marry her, which he eventually does. Women sighed, men cried and the movie became a box office hit.

A few years later, a 40-year-old man rapes a 13-year-old girl and then pays her parents to marry her. Might he have seen the same movie and thought that was the way to handle things?

Another movie had the female protagonist raped at the end, and the perpetrator going scot-free. When I asked the Censor Board, in a separate meeting, why they let that go, their reply was 'because she was a gossip!'. There was total silence when I reminded them that in our country, rape is a crime.

When people who are supposed to uphold the law ignore it, they have no right to lecture the public about not adhering to it. Just recently an ex-senator, someone who for a time helped to make our laws, told a woman that even if she gave him 'unlimited freedom', he wouldn't rape her.

Outrage exploded on Twitter but not in the mainstream

media. How does a former lawmaker talk like that? Does he think that women would be grateful if he raped them? And therefore by refusing to, he was insulting her? Obviously he thought his lower appendage was more powerful than his brain.

The fact that the word 'rape' floats so easily out of someone's mouth, especially a former lawmaker's, and that movie scriptwriters think nothing of making rape an unpunished part of the plot, points to something very disturbing: that there are a lot of people who think nothing about rape, and that they confuse it with sex. Sex is a mutually consensual act of love. Rape on the other hand does not involve mutual consent, and is often a violent act. Statutory rape assumes that a young girl, still legally defined as a child, just doesn't know what she is doing, even if she seemingly consented to it.

I wonder how these judges, politicians and movie directors would feel if it was their daughters or sisters that were in the same dilemma? Would they be so forgiving because the rapist had a supposedly brighter future than the victim? What if it was the victim who had the bright but now extinguished future?

*12 September 2014*

## A Deeper Look at Horrific Crimes

Last week was a particularly horrific and sad week in our country. A man abused to death his toddler stepson. A killer made a little girl his gruesome victim. Ten men and boys raped a teenage girl, and the mother of another teenager who was raped by two men, whipped one of the men in public.

And if these horrors were not bad enough, a little girl accidentally fell to her death in a shopping mall.

Most of us would be forgiven for thinking that the entire country needs a flower bath, to get rid of what seems to be a dark cloud hovering over us.

But maybe we are not far wrong, because there do seem to be bad vibes over our land, fuelled by so much aggravation, angst and animosity among us. Perhaps we are spending so much time arguing over things that don't really matter that we have neglected what really does matter.

And what does matter? For one thing, the safety of our people, especially our women and children matters very much. Every time something as dreadful as child abuse, rape or murder happens, a huge outcry ensues and many newspaper column inches are written anguishing about it, with calls for ever-more severe punishment for perpetrators. Indeed perpetrators must be caught and punished so that we all feel safe again. Let us not forget that the killer of little Nurin Jazlin has never been caught. But let's also do more about prevention.

Prevention involves investigating and understanding the circumstances under which these crimes happen. Do people really wake up and think of killing their children that day? Or, is that the tragic result of a build-up of stresses and strains that could have been mitigated if only there was help? Could a rape by people known to a victim have been averted, by more vigilant neighbours directly or indirectly by an environment that was different? If the mother of the murdered child had not been homeless, would the child have fallen prey to the killer so easily?

I really wish our media would probe into these cases a bit more deeply. What would cause a whole group of men and boys to band together to rape that young girl? It was reported that they were high on drugs. What goes on in that village that there can be so many men taking drugs and assaulting girls with impunity? Is there a larger problem here of unemployment, boredom and repression? In the wake of Elliot Rodger's mass murders, there were a lot of articles analysing his motivations and mental state. I wish there was also the same for not just this gang rape but also the others, to see if there are some underlying causes for this violence. Without knowing these, how would we prevent them?

With the child who died of abuse, once again we should look at the back story. There can never be an excuse for child battery, but when you look at a young twice-married mother with many children, you can see how the stresses of such circumstances may make a person snap. Not all young parents abuse their children, but very often those who do abuse their kids tend to have married and had their children at a young age. Perhaps they were married off to prevent illicit sex, with no contraceptive advice and little preparation for parenthood. This particular mother was only 31 and the dead child, aged six, was her fourth. Did her husband find the needs of her children taking away her attention from him? To me, it's yet another reason not to allow young people to marry before they are ready for the many responsibilities of marriage and parenthood.

The background of the mother of the murdered child is also a sad tale. Her husband in prison, she was left with three young children and no way of caring for them. Leaving two with relatives, she was left homeless with her youngest and spent all her time wandering the city and living on the generosity of friends. Where is our Welfare Department for vulnerable families of prisoners like these? When we send men to prison, do we check on how their families would survive? Or don't we care?

Our many social problems need to be examined in a much more holistic way than they are now. But that takes intelligence, leadership and compassion. There can't be anything more callous than a minister who blames homelessness on the 'generosity of Malaysians', as if to live on the dangerous streets is a lifestyle choice. Perhaps she should spend a night serving at soup kitchens.

As long as such arrogant blindness prevails, we will never solve these problems. And the violence will continue.

*6 June 2014*

# Security and Insecurity

Since we are all worried about security these days, I decided to look up the meaning of 'insecurity'. Besides the feeling of being constantly in danger or under threat, insecurity also means 'a feeling of uncertainty, or a lack of confidence and anxiety about yourself'.

While we worry daily about the many crimes being committed in our neighbourhoods with no real solution in sight, sometimes I wonder if we have a security crisis or an insecurity crisis. While it is true that security is a constant issue, I wonder if the real reason behind it is that feeling of uncertainty or a lack of confidence and anxiety about ourselves.

These feelings of security and insecurity are of course related. On the one hand, the very people who should make us feel secure are in fact making us insecure. How certain do we feel about our futures when we see hesitant and sometimes absent leadership at times when we most need it? How can we not feel anxious when the leadership is silent on the things that matter to the citizenry?

As a citizen, I want a decent life for my family, my fellow citizens and myself. This, anyone would think, is quite basic and common to everyone. I want to be able to have a roof over my head, education for my kids, the opportunity to earn a decent living and affordable healthcare when I need it. When a human being is unable to have these basics, then they start to feel that most normal of human instincts, insecurity. If enough people feel that way, then that's a recipe for instability and mass insecurity.

It is not possible for any country to be stable if many of its people feel hungry or deprived of the most essential ingredients to lead a normal life. Countries rise and fall based on these simple facts. Once inequalities start to spread, then it is only normal that insecurity, in the sense of danger, follows.

I was talking to a friend who has been working abroad a lot about a situation that he found very stark since he's been back. There are people who seem to be caught in a quagmire of debt that they simply cannot get out of. The vicious cycle of inability to access what a person needs which leads to overuse of credit which leads to an inability to pay which then leads to getting loans at high interest from unscrupulous persons seems never ending. It leads to insecurity not just for the original borrower but also for all those within his or her family circles.

Recently, two leading religious figures have spoken about this terrible crisis that many face, of easy credit and crushing debt. The former Archbishop of Canterbury, Dr Rowan Williams, warned that the ease with which money, in its virtual form, not in exchange for actual goods and services, is available has led to much misery among people. Most recently, Pope Francis talked about the same thing, how the pursuit of money for its own sake, has brought with it 'a culture where the weakest in society suffered the most and often, those on the fringes "fall away", including the elderly, who he said were victims of a "hidden euthanasia" caused by neglect of those no longer considered productive'.

I have yet to hear the Muslim equivalent of this, of concern for a global system that is increasing insecurity of people everywhere. Instead I hear of a different insecurity, one in which there are constant so-called moral attacks, usually by imagined assailants. Where limited interpretations of religion are to be enforced because otherwise the religion will disappear, despite evidence to the contrary.

In some ways, these self-appointed guardians of religion have reason to worry. Every action of theirs is self-defeating. For every cruelty they inflict on those who are weak, they lose more adherents. For every injustice they perpetuate, there are people who leave disgusted. For every justification they give to inequality, people balk and root for equality.

When we look at the most unstable countries in the world, inevitably they are also the ones with masses of poor people. Economic injustice breeds problems not just within countries, but externally as well. It leads to mass migrations of people to look for work, and sometimes it brings violence. It thus makes sense to prioritise dealing with such injustice.

Instead we see our leaders behaving like people anxious about protecting their own comforts rather than anyone else's. This they do by distracting us from real issues, by telling us that some small groups of people, even dead ones, are a threat, by refusing to let some people speak or even be seen in our media.

So I have to ask: who's the insecure one?

*30 September 2013*

# The Inequality of Freedoms

I've been noticing a disturbing phenomenon recently among my brethren. It is a type of mob behaviour where groups of people will attack online a person, usually female, accusing her of immorality based totally on something superficial, usually her dress. It happened with the gymnast who was criticised for her regulation gymastics leotard instead of cheered for her gold medal. And it happened again when a seven-year-old girl was taken to task for wearing a two-piece bathing suit while on holiday with her parents.

To attack a little girl with an as-yet unformed body who was holidaying with her parents seemed to me to be beyond reason. There is something else going on here besides the apparent self-righteousness. If one wants to seem devout and to admonish someone for supposed unIslamic behaviour, there are recommended ways to do it. Online slut-shaming isn't one of them.

I'm no psychologist, but it is interesting to me that as our society gets more 'religious' (at least by some people's definitions), there is increasing mob behaviour against anyone deemed to not fit into those definitions. Sadly our authorities' idea of religiously correct behaviour involves more restrictions every day. Their key word is 'don't', rather than 'do'. Thus people are told every day of the things they must not do if they are keen to end up in heaven. Apparently there is a list of 70 major sins that we can do to ensure that we go to the wrong place. Odd, considering I was brought up to understand that Islam is a very easy religion with very few major sins, defaming people being one of them.

When people are told daily that they cannot do so many things, and yet they see that some people can freely do them, then resentments mount. How is it that some people can wear what they want but I cannot? How is it that some people can do what they want but I cannot?

What we thus have is an inequality of freedoms, and I believe this is closely tied to the inequality of wealth in this country. If you have money, you are likely to go to better schools, have more job opportunities, travel more and buy whatever you want. The world is pretty much open to you. If you don't, then you have none of these options.

The income inequalities in this country are well documented. Not only is there a huge swathe of people with very low incomes in this country but the gap between them and the very wealthy is getting bigger. But not a lot is being done to narrow these gaps, apart from giving the poor handouts which are one-offs and unsustainable. Besides, as the saying goes, they don't teach a man to fish.

Thus the way to assuage the feelings of those at the bottom is by telling them that while they may not have much, their advantage is that they are more likely to go to heaven. Rich people are apparently more prone to sinning, so be happy that you are poor but heading in the right direction. Hence the poor spend what they have on the right rituals, the right clothes, making sure their children are well-educated religiously if nothing else. They will be rewarded some day, they are promised.

But meanwhile the bills need to be paid. The kids are getting nowhere because the schools are not preparing them for a productive life. Food and public transport are getting more and more expensive. The GST hits them harder.

Still our politicians and ulama tell us salvation is at hand if only we keep on that straight and very narrow path. It's hard going but we believe in them. Even when it's clear that there's not much joy in our every day lives.

Meanwhile how is it that some of our brethren have the freedoms that we don't have? How is it that they can go on holidays abroad and buy fancy clothes, not all of which are shariah-compliant? How is it that they can smile and laugh with impunity? Aren't they afraid of going to hell by enjoying heaven on earth?

Thus the mob behaviour happens. How to justify someone else's freedoms except to cast them as being sinful? It doesn't matter if they are innocent children, they have to be as suppressed as our children are. Only then can there be equality in oppression, the logic goes.

Politicians may not notice this, and may even encourage this as a cover-up for their failures. But if the inequalities in income are not addressed, the inequalities in freedoms will continue to breed ever greater resentments and who knows where this will lead to.

Something to ponder on this 31 August. Are all our people equally *merdeka*?

*27 August 2015*

# The Dangers of Racial Stereotyping

When I was a student in the UK, one of the most hated politicians then was Enoch Powell who was constantly railing against immigration in Britain, claiming that it would alter the British 'character'. Powell was so strident with his views expressing them in his now-infamous 'Rivers of Blood' speech that his own Conservative Party, despite years of service that had enabled the party to win elections, eventually sacked him.

This was in a country that, unlike ours, values freedom of speech. Yet the party felt that someone as extreme as Powell could not be a member anymore, not if it wanted to move forward in an inevitably changing nation. He could say what he wanted but outside the party.

We too have been known to sack people whose views did not comply with what the heads of the party regarded as theirs. This is not the same as censoring them, only that they had to do it outside. Thus the dignity of the party remains intact, not tainted by what they regarded as aberrations.

No doubt, sometimes regarding people as aberrations may be unjust because in fact they represent views that simply differ from the norm. But dealing with such issues clearly gives everyone else an idea of what the norms and aberration are. Not dealing with it, however, creates confusion and raises the possibility that maybe the aberration is not one at all, but in fact just the public expression of the norm.

We fought so long not to stereotype our people according to race by increasing educational and economic opportunities. Yet we still see it happening. In local schools, children are pushed into certain sports not by ability but purely by race. Thus Punjabis must play hockey and not chess. Malays must play football and not tennis, while Chinese must only play badminton. Is it any wonder that they don't excel in any sport? You have to wonder where the powers-that-be in that school got their ideas from, *Mein Kampf*?

When we talk about race, we make the mistake of lumping together a whole bunch of human beings, with all their individual quirks, whims and fancies, into what we think is a cohesive body. But it is not. If anything, sometimes race is the most tenuous thing that holds us together.

I may have told this story before. A long time ago, as I rushed through a crowded London Underground, an old Jewish man stopped me. Taking his handkerchief out, he insisted that there was something on my jacket. It took me a while to understand that the man had seen someone spit on me and was now offering his handkerchief to clean the spittle off.

It was then that I became aware of the awful silent insidiousness of racism, that someone could have displayed such hatred on a total stranger, based entirely on colour of skin. In a way, I should be thankful it was only spit and not something worse.

On the other hand, the same incident made me realise that while there is evil, there can also be much good. I was also a stranger to the old man but he saw me as a human being entitled to respect and dignity. Thus he empathised with the injustice that was done to me and sought to restore my dignity by offering his handkerchief for me to clean up. He asked for nothing in return and indeed disappeared into the crowds soon after with not a word more.

When we talk about race, we talk about groups of people, a homogenous faceless group defined by general characteristics that we think of as applicable to all of them. But on a day-to-day basis, it is not the race that matters but the human being that we are dealing with.

I had one of those telemarketing calls offering free medical checkups the other day. Disturbed by it, I started to question the caller for details. The woman was undoubtedly of the same race as me. But the sheer rudeness and unprofessionalism of her responses showed that she had no respect whatsoever for the person she was calling or for her own company or job. Did it matter what race she was? No, what mattered was that she was unable to make a connection with another human being, even when she claimed to be offering something ostensibly good for me.

Given a choice between these two people, I would sooner take the old man to tea than this woman. He and I have a common respect for human beings that she did not, despite our common ethnicity. Was he the aberration or she? Since I believe that it is human to be kind, I prefer to believe she is.

*10 September 2008*

# Be Proactive to Eradicate Racism

Some months ago I had an interesting session with some young people belonging to an evangelical youth movement. Our conversation was about stereotypes. At the heart of racism, I said, are stereotypes about people because they belong to one race or religion. And the thing to remember about stereotypes is, every time you stereotype someone, someone else somewhere is stereotyping you.

I've been talking about racism all last week. Prof. Aneez Esmail gave a talk about how Britain has handled race relations at a public forum and a closed roundtable session. In both cases, we Malaysians proved that, aside from politicians, we are quite capable of discussing race with maturity and rationality.

Prof. Aneez stressed that he was not here to tell us how to conduct race relations in Malaysia. Rather he was relating his own experience of racism as an immigrant to Britain and how he went about challenging it. His challenges led to recognition of much institutional racism in the medical profession and at universities. Empirical evidence about the racism was key to his success. He proved that hospitals were ten times more likely to offer jobs to applicants with white names than to those with non-white names. A similar study in Australia published only recently showed the same thing among employers there.

The issue of racism is considered so sensitive in this country that the general prescription is that we should not talk about it.

This has only led to mounting tensions when problems remain unresolved. Ironically politicians are not censored in the same way as others, even though they seem to be the ones least likely to be capable of rational discussion. As a result, they have led to even more heightening of tensions.

Having said that, I believe that many of us are sincere in wanting to grapple with the issue of racism all round. Everyone feels hard done by in one way or another, whether officially or unofficially.

Prof. Aneez stressed that we all live with multiple identities. I am not just Malay or Muslim, I am also a woman, a wife, mother, daughter, activist and whatever else I do and am. So to stereotype through one shared identity does not do justice to every individual. All Muslims in the world may share some common beliefs but not all common traits. Not all men are chauvinists. Not all Chinese are hardworking. Not all Indians can sing like Shah Rukh Khan, and so on.

The point is when we group people under one single shared identity, we invariably label them with the worst traits of that identity. Worse still, we then refuse to recognise the good in the other identities that they carry. Thus when we have prejudices against one group of people, we ignore the individual good traits that they might have under their other identities. We might dislike someone just because we have prejudices against their race while ignoring what they may have done for charity or their expertise in their jobs, for example.

The other point is that when we say we want to eradicate racism, we must mean that for everyone. We cannot accuse someone else of racism while not recognising it in ourselves. What's more, we cannot reject racism among our fellow citizens but allow it against foreigners. Why is it OK to hurl epithets at Indonesians, Africans and Bangladeshis when it is not at Malaysian Malays, Chinese or Indians? Racism is racism, no matter whom it is directed at.

While we are reflecting on how we may solve our internal racial issues, we must also reflect on why it is that we stereotype all Indonesians as criminals, all Africans as thugs and all Bangladeshis as poor labourers. And why it is that we are not ashamed of ourselves when we do this. Perhaps we don't realise that over in Indonesia, all Malaysians are stereotyped as cruel and inhumane? Africans think we have something against black people. And in Bangladesh, as much as they admire Malaysia, they also wonder why we treat their people so badly. Stereotypes don't take into account that individuals may think differently; they tar everyone with the same brush.

Prof. Aneez pointed out that it is not possible to totally eradicate racism but we can do a lot to make it socially disapproved of. We can take pro-active measures to mitigate the impact of institutional racism with time-limited quotas and affirmative action. For example, we could introduce affirmative action to bring in more non-Malays into the civil service and police force with special incentives as well as punitive measures for non-compliance by those institutions. The lack of candidates cannot be an excuse but an unacceptable lack of effort.

All we need is political will. And therein lies the problem.

*29 June 2009*

# Racist Stories Persist

Having been brought up always to be polite, I can be quite shocked when people are rude and direct. Once many years ago, an American woman asked me how it felt to be an oppressed Muslim woman. After getting over my shock, I put it down to sheer ignorance.

Not long after, a Russian man, ostensibly well educated, asked me why Muslims liked to cut off their enemies' heads. I'm not sure how I managed to contain myself but it did give me an insight into how some people have no idea how their words can sound to others.

Since those days I have managed to develop much better shock-absorbers and few things manage to rattle me as before. I have heard people blithely ask me why we don't simply kill all people with HIV as a way of containing the epidemic, as if they were giving me a bright idea to solve a simple problem. In all seriousness someone also told me that the reason why black people don't excel at swimming is because their skin pigments are so heavy it is difficult for them to float.

All these people genuinely believed that they were imparting wisdom. It never occurred to them that they might sound totally out of synch with the times, where racist and genocidal ideas no longer hold currency.

Still it is rare for me to hear anything so shocking anymore. Most people I know would never stereotype or judge others by the colour of their skin, their race or their religion. We take everyone as equals and value them for their talents, skills and ethics.

It thus becomes a major shock to me to find that outside that circle, the world is different. Reading headlines in some local newspapers I find myself disturbed by the blatantly racist stories that pass for news. While such outright racism towards fellow Malaysians is not yet considered de rigeur, foreigners are easy targets, especially if they don't come from countries more developed than us. Whole continents of people are deemed criminal with impunity and racist epithets trip off tongues and pages as easily as praise for politicians.

When I remark on this, people defend the racism. The media, they say, are just stating 'facts' about some people whom 'we all know' tend to commit crimes. It never seems to occur to anyone to question these 'facts', any more than it occurs to right-wing Americans to question the 'fact' that Muslims are all terrorists and spend all our time stoning people.

To say that the media is only reflecting what people think is to hide behind a disingenuous bush. The media both reflects and creates stereotypes. Indeed it reinforces them, and then refuses to take responsibility for any violence that may result. An Indiana man who was charged with setting fire to an Islamic centre said that the only Muslims he knew were those he saw on Fox News, a channel that doesn't bother to hide its prejudice against Muslims. Similarly highly distorted news on the LGBT community in Malaysia has resulted in some of them suffering violence at the hands of thugs.

Let's not even mention the things that some Malaysians get away with saying on social media. There are those who claim to belong to a religion of peace, yet happily spew the most vicious anonymous diatribes against those of other faiths. Worse this is done in the name of their own faith.

The result is a lot of counter-prejudice and stereotypes. My people, the people I knew growing up as infinitely polite, gentle and considerate, are these days labelled uncouth, intolerant, aggressive and hypocritical. Just because a few people are intemperate in their language, all of us are labeled thugs and louts. Worse still, those who strut around with an air of unwarranted superiority claim to represent all of us.

If my fellow citizens feel hurt by the actions of these few, I feel hurt too. My people are being labelled haters and bridge-burners when throughout history we have been the most accommodating and hospitable of people. Because of a few bad examples, all of us have to suffer from sometimes barely concealed condescension. And racism breeds racism; some people only know to respond to hate with even more hate.

Since our leaders fail dismally to delineate between what is right and what is so patently wrong, it is left to civil society, especially young people, to find ways of making a peaceful point. Last Sunday we sat under shady trees and read books to enlighten our friends and ourselves. And with that, rose above the muck and saw one another clearly for the human beings that we are.

*2 February 2013*

# Lessons from the Paris Terror Attacks

Just when we thought the year might get off to a good start, Paris happened. In three days, 20 people were killed; 12 in the original attack, five hostages in two related incidents and three of the assailants. By any measure this was a terrible tragedy, causing pain and suffering to all the families of the dead and injured.

Sadly it will also cause lasting pain to the French Muslim community in particular and all Muslims elsewhere in general because, once again, the entire community has been linked unjustly with extremism and violence.

Debates now rage about the value of freedom of speech. Some people say that in any democratic society we must have freedom of speech including the freedom to offend. Others say that it is that very freedom of speech that has led to this violence.

Like most things in life, the answer probably lies in between. Some commentators have pointed out that while satire is certainly part and parcel of a democratic society, it is usually aimed at the powerful as a way of pointing out their foibles and abuses. True satire that aims to bring justice in society never targets the weak and marginalised, voiceless people who look to others to bring their problems to society's attention. As one tweet brilliantly put it, 'I think satire should be a punch aimed up at the powerful, not a blow rained down on the weak.' I wonder sometimes what would happen if some of our rabid supremacists decided to launch a satirical magazine to draw cartoons of minorities in this country.

On the other hand, there are comments from some people that events like *Charlie Hebdo* 'prove' that we need the Sedition Act. This is simply another way of saying that those journalists deserve to be killed because they were asking for it. If France had had a Sedition Act, they reason, then the magazine would have been stopped much earlier from drawing those cartoons, and the French Muslims would have been happy, despite being marginalised, suffering from poverty, unemployment and all the other things that generally breed disgruntlement. We seem to have a propensity to blame the victims for their troubles, much like we blame women who get raped for the way they dress or for being out at night.

I'm not sure how the Sedition Act that targets people talking and writing about local issues is going to stop Malaysians from going to join ISIS, arguably the most serious danger we now face.

Perhaps some people did not notice that the first policeman who was killed, brutally shot in the head as he lay wounded, was a Muslim called Ahmed Merabet. In a moving tribute to his dead brother, Malek Merabet said, 'My brother was Muslim and he was killed by two terrorists, by two false Muslims … Islam is a religion of peace and love. As far as my brother's death is concerned it was a waste. He was very proud of the name Ahmed Merabet, proud to represent the police and of defending the values of the Republic – liberty, equality, fraternity.'

More than anything, Ahmed Merabet underscored what this was really about. That this was a killing of French people by French people, not of non-Muslims by Muslims. Just as at one time Northern Irish people killed other Northern Irish people. Undoubtedly one set of people felt disgruntled by treatment from the other and a small number decided that violence was to be their response. To then tar an entire community, as if every single member is a likely killer, is surely compounding the injustice.

Framing this tragedy entirely in Muslim/non-Muslim terms is of no use when life is much more complicated than that. Not only was one of the murdered policemen Muslim, so was one of the employees of the Jewish grocery where two gunmen held hostages. Lassan Bathily was hailed a hero for saving the lives of several hostages by hiding them in a freezer room. Malek Merabet made the same point: 'I address myself now to all the racists, Islamophobes and antisemites. One must not confuse extremists with Muslims. Mad people have neither colour or religion.'

Which is a really pertinent point. Only mad people think that the way to solve problems is to gun down a bunch of cartoonists. On the other hand, it is also not reasonable to clamp down on people who are already downtrodden, or who already have no outlet to air their grouses and not expect some form of reaction. We should perhaps be thankful that in our country this reaction only comes in the form of peaceful demonstrations, articles and Facebook comments.

The real lesson to be learnt from the *Charlie Hebdo* tragedy is that inequality has consequences. But that may be lost on some people.

*15 January 2015*

# Restrictions on Democracy

When did 'democracy' become a dirty word?

In all the past 55 years, we have been proud of being a democracy, minimalist though it may be. We elect our Parliament like clockwork every five years or so and everyone is aware that that is the first hurdle they have to get over in order to get into power.

Of course, we have a far-from-perfect democracy but then there are no perfect ones anywhere. We could do with a more inclusive and representative government and certainly could do with a more vibrant and free media and more space for alternative viewpoints to be heard.

Still we like to describe our federation with its constitutional monarchy as a democracy, our democracy.

So it rather surprises me that, of late, there are voices that seem to say that democracy is a bad thing to have. For some reason, there are people who think that an elected form of government where people have the power to choose who they want to elect them is not a good thing. Perhaps this is because they are unsure that this type of government will put them into power at all. Some are even going so far as to say that democracy is incompatible with our state religion, Islam. That's rather odd because I've just been at a conference where an Islamic scholar stated that Islam is the most democratic of religions, because everyone has equal access to God. Yet, he added, most Muslims live in undemocratic states.

This sudden turn in attitudes against democracy has had predictable results. Anyone who talks about democracy is suddenly viewed with suspicion, as if they are advocating that the Devil himself should take over the country. People's right to voice critical opinions is suddenly seen as traitorous. The possibility of alternative administrations is deemed taboo, a word that has connotations beyond the mundanity of voting, rather like talking about sex is considered taboo. If the citizens of a country are not allowed to elect whom they want, then they don't live in a democracy. So to say that it is taboo to elect anyone other than the present government is to bring the conversation to a realm that is beyond rational argument.

Somehow nowadays it is a sin to get our people to think democratically, as if democracy is a religion that teaches immorality. Teaching citizens their rights as citizens is now seen as almost a crime, warranting investigation into every aspect that might conceivably unearth some wrongdoing. Those who promote democracy are suddenly seen as foreign agents. This is rather odd, since there are many people who promote anti-democracy in this country who are also funded by foreigners.

I remember in my childhood being taught about democracy at school. My teachers would talk about how concepts like apartheid or 'the colour bar' were undemocratic. We held mock elections where we would have candidates and campaigns, including 'political' rallies, so that we would understand the whole process of how our leaders are elected. Of great importance were the issues our 'candidates' put up; those who had the best solutions to our issues at school were the ones who would get elected.

Today I hear that schools are not encouraged to have any

such thing in case our children get 'funny' ideas. Instead we are differentiating children by the way they look and dress, rather than treating all of them as equal. We expose them to possible discrimination, even violence, even though our Federal Constitution says that every citizen has an equal right to education.

Every day we have new restrictions on our already limited democracy. We can get arrested for comments we never made just because someone made them on our website or Facebook page. Some of us, in an already limited job market, find ourselves charged with allegedly working against our own religion even though we are not responsible for anything other than doing our jobs.

Even though both our official religion and Constitution gives us rights, these rights are now contested. And contested in such a way that those who shout loudest win, even if their numbers are small. Yet these same folks would be the first to demand their right to speak should anyone object to what they say.

We need to ask ourselves, how did we come to this state where democracy is confused with 'total freedom' and 'Westernisation'? Is the West the only ones who are allowed democracy? In that case, why are thousands of people in those autocratic Middle Eastern countries demanding to have a say in how their countries are run? Are they all unIslamic?

Are we somehow undeserving of democracy, of the simple right to have a say?

*27 September 2012*

# The Hidden Hands Fallacy

Let me first wish everyone Selamat Hari Raya, *maaf zahir batin*. This Ramadan has been a particularly sad one with the MH17 tragedy, especially when it came so soon after the disappearance of MH370. Our hearts and prayers go to all those who lost their loved ones in both tragedies.

But even without MH17, Ramadan was no less rancourous with attempts to ban soup kitchens and bad-tempered drivers behaving without restraint towards old people*. Then in a misplaced attempt to be 'even-handed', some radio stations made the perpetrator look like a celebrity, much to the disgust of many.

Whatever it was, a month that is supposed to be about restraint and moderation turned out to be ill-tempered. I can't help thinking that if it hadn't been for the very sobering effect of MH17, things would have been much worse.

Not that we can truly expect the rest of the year to be calm and peaceful. Already there are people, whose sole purpose in life seems to be as divisive as possible, who have declared that democracy is an evil invention of the West that we should not follow. Its worst effect, it seems, is that it gives 'citizens the right to determine their own future'. Funny, I thought that's why we wanted independence from our colonisers, so that we could decide the future of our country for ourselves.

But I suppose their argument here is that we are still not independent because there are many 'hidden hands' actually steering our path. The thing about these 'hidden hands' is that apparently they operate through us being a democratic nation where we get to vote our leaders into power and also have a say in what we want for our country. Thus an undemocratic concept like the 'hidden hands' operates through being democratic. So if we didn't have democracy, their logic goes, these invisible unknown hands wouldn't control us.

The funny thing is there must be a lot of these unseen hands around the world since there are so many democratic countries. If they vote in the people we like, then the hidden hands fail. But when they vote in people we don't like, then those hands managed to win. Since it is democracy that works in both cases, it's hard not to think that those hands are really inconsistent. So perhaps we should follow the undemocratic nations where the hands are not hidden at all, like, for example, Saudi Arabia?

So after 57 years of democracy, more or less, there are now people who think this is not a good idea. Not that they have any idea what should replace it, apart from that we should have an 'Islamic' state. But a true Muslim state is a democratic one. Indeed the Qur'an warns us against despots and tyrants.

In chapter 4, verse 135, the Holy Book says 'O You who have attained to faith! Be ever steadfast in upholding equity, bearing witness to the truth for the sake of God, even though it be against your own selves or your parents and kinsfolk. Whether the person concerned be rich or poor, God's claim takes precedence over [the claims of] either of them.  Do not, then, follow your own desires, lest you swerve from justice: for if you distort [the truth], behold, God is indeed aware of all that you do!' (Translation by Assad.)

There are some whose sense of history seems to have little to do with facts. The constitutional monarchy, they claim, existed long before we became independent. Which is an interesting re-telling of history, given that we did not have a Constitution before independence. So what was 'constitutional' about the sultanates before then? Is that what they are proposing we revert to?

There are others who claim we should not have democracy because our Federal Constitution doesn't contain the word. I do love selective literalists who don't know their history. Did our forefathers clamour for independence because they wanted to be under anyone else's yoke? Why on earth did they decide we should have a Parliament we should vote for in elections if they did not want democracy? Did they have to spell out every single word or did they know that 'self-determination' meant democracy and nothing else? Perhaps people in 1957 were more intelligent than today?

And as for claiming we should not have democracy because it's not mentioned in our Federal Constitution, I find this disingenuous of the selective literalists.

After all they're quite happy to want to do things that aren't mentioned in the Qur'an. Like, the punishment for apostasy or for drinking. Or to do the opposite of things enjoined in the Qur'an such as not respecting people's privacy and raiding them in their homes.

*31 July 2014*

*See 'Young woman attacks elderly man's car with steering lock after accident', *The Star*, 16 July 2014.

# Choice Versus Opinion

These days if you walk into a coffee bar, you find yourself faced with an overwhelming variety of choices. You can have strong, weak, with milk, without milk, several different types of milk and in several sizes. It can be confusing but eventually you make a choice, even if it is for the simplest version possible.

The point of the modern coffee bar is that you have choices and you can decide yourself, even if it is to finally just walk out without ordering anything.

But how to do you make these choices? For a first-timer, the variety can be just too much and some guidance from someone would be helpful. But as you get more educated about the coffee, eventually you become confident enough to know what you like and make your own decision.

These days we are faced with choices in almost every area of our life. We can choose to do many things or to do nothing. We can choose to do useful things or waste our time. We can choose to wear bright colours or dull ones. Every single waking minute we make choices on where to go and what to do.

We can also make choices concerning what we think about things. And yet somehow when we make our choices about our thoughts, we put less consideration into them than we do for choosing coffee, or cars.

When we are in a situation where we have to make a choice, we consider many things. If we need to choose a mobile phone to buy, we'll read up about it, ask friends for their opinions and eventually decide on one which both suits our needs and our wallets. We will take our time to make the decision that is right for us.

Whether we are making choices about where to eat, where to go on holiday, what insurance to buy or who to marry, we think a lot about them.

Yet when it comes to having an opinion about something, we spend much less time. We read headlines and short articles and already decide that we know what to think about something. The media, especially TV and our mainstream papers, tell us what to think about some issues and we accept their directions with very little questioning. It doesn't seem to occur to us that like everything else, we have a choice in what we think about many things and the choices can be as varied as coffee.

But there are so many of us who believe that we have no choice in our thoughts. Whether out of laziness or fear, we follow the way others, or our leaders, say we should think because we don't realise that even in this we have choices. We may well come to the same conclusion but we never think that we should go through the same decision-making process as we do for all other choices in our lives.

And yet we think of ourselves as autonomous human beings with the faculty to make independent decisions. It always astounds me how many people use the same words to talk about things as our leaders and media use. Few people seem to realise that they can actually use a vocabulary that is bigger than what is given to them. Instead they limit themselves to the same words, which in effect means they also limit their own thinking about the issue.

This is why when people disagree with something, their arguments are often so limited. Despite facts that can prove otherwise, they continue to use the same arguments over and over again, as if continued repetition will one day make it come true. To find new facts or to be more creative with what they already know is too hard for some, or they think there is no other choice but to think the way they always have.

Perhaps it is a consequence of our less-than-stellar education system in which our children are told that their choices are limited to only whatever their teachers tell them. It is a system that insists that the only right choice is to obey authority regardless of whether they are doing the right thing or not. So our kids grow up not realising that there are many more choices in the world, and that the best ones are perhaps the ones they are never told about.

Fifty-seven years after independence, our people live in this mistaken belief that they have the agency to make all the choices they need to make. But in fact every single day their choices are narrowed, instilled mostly by fear.

We blind ourselves to this situation because we think our leaders are making the right choices for us.

But what if they aren't?

*11 January 2014*

## Protest Not for Protest's Sake

On 29 August, Malaysians proved something very important, that it is possible to come together in common cause and do it peacefully. No more can we believe anyone who says that any gathering of more than five people is bound to be disorderly and violent.

Bersih 4 proved that people can be disciplined and orderly in big crowds. They obeyed instructions not to breach the barriers at Dataran Merdeka and they cleaned up afterwards. In between they marched, they put up posters to express their feelings about current issues, they made and listened to speeches, they sang, they camped out and they ate. And they did all this peacefully, in great caramaderie with one another.

This time I could not be in the country to join my fellow citizens in protest. Instead I joined some 1000 Malaysians in London on the same day to demonstrate for the same cause. We started off in front of our High Commission where people held up banners and posters and listened to a few speeches, waved at High Commission officials and then walked to Whitehall where we stopped near Downing Street, before ending up at Trafalgar Square where we sang 'NegaraKu' in the rain. There were only two policemen watching over us, which again proved that we don't need a big police presence to ensure that we behaved.

In some 40 cities all over the world, Malaysians gathered for Bersih, all without incident. It just goes to show that violence at protests is not caused by protestors but by the use of teargas and watercannons. We have to commend the police for realising this simple fact this time.

Now there is talk of a counter-rally, which has already been declared illegal but which insists, like Bersih, to carry on anyway. I am all for freedom of speech, so generally, no matter how despicable, I would not stop anyone from expressing their opinions.

The trouble is I have a problem trying to figure out what the so-called Red Shirts stand for. They seem to want to protest for the sake of protesting against protestors, specifically Bersih protestors. But while we are clear about the issues that Bersih espouses, we don't really know what the Red Shirts are spoiling for a fight for.

I suppose it's fair to assume that since the Red Shirt Rally is anti-Bersih, then they must want the opposite of whatever Bersih's 200,000 participants want. Let's look at what this is:

Bersih wants free and fair elections. I suppose the Red Shirts must therefore want unfree and unfair elections, possibly the only way any of them can hold any public position. If they were fluent in English, I would recommend their slogan be 'Stack the Deck'.

Secondly, Bersih 4 is demanding a clean government. It must therefore mean that the Red Shirts are demanding a dirty government, one in which money decides everything from who gets to govern to what policies and laws are made. I wonder how many Reds actually think they will have a say in any government policies, given that few of them are likely to be millionaires. Millionaires don't need BR1M.

Speaking of which, Bersih 4's third demand is for action to save our economy. As our ringgit plummets to depths never seen before and everything becomes extremely expensive for us, obviously we need to see concrete moves being taken to ensure that we don't become relegated to 'least developed country' status. But since the Red Shirts are taking issue with Bersih, I must assume that they won't mind if our country descends to a level on par with some of the poorest countries in the world. Maybe they hope to go abroad to find work like some of our neighbours.

Fourthly, Bersih 4 is demanding the right to dissent. This means the right to disagree, respectfully, with anyone, including the government. Since the Red Shirts are already exercising their right to disagree with Bersih, they really should not have any problems with this demand. However, I do think that the right to dissent means having a vocabulary that contains more than one word – 'stupid' – to describe those you don't like.

So on 16 September, the Red Shirts would like to emulate Bersih by having their own 'illegal' rally on a day meant to celebrate our unity in diversity. I don't know how the Reds intend to express diversity since thus far they have looked monoracial and monogendered. And unity with yourself doesn't really count for much.

Perhaps on Malaysia Day we should all just stay home and watch the breaking-bricks-with-your-head display from afar. Or attend other fun events elsewhere. They can bring their own food and drink from home. And let's see if they'll clean up afterwards.

*9 September 2015*

# Broken Taboos

In the past week we've seen many taboos being broken. The taboo against assembling in public to demonstrate was of course already broken some time ago but until last week it was taboo for any pro-government people to do the same.

Then there was the taboo on laying hands on the police. That was broken too when red-shirted demonstrators last week injured some policemen because they were stopped from going into a certain area of KL. Of course some people immediately disassociated themselves from these unruly demonstrators, a privilege they didn't allow anyone from Bersih to do.

Then there was the taboo against calling people names. When I was little, the Malay word for pig was considered something nobody well brought-up ever mentioned in polite company. This has stood for so long that someone decided to substitute it with the Arabic word 'khinzir' just so you could talk about the same animal without offending anyone's sensibilities.

Last week that taboo was broken when some two-bit barbequed fishseller called a whole community pigs, obviously with the intention of insulting them and then disingenuously explaining that it can't be offensive since the target community loves eating it. What would be the point of insulting people with supposedly non-insulting words?

Then some genius broke yet another taboo, by associating his religion with something not just negative but despicably so.

These would be the same people who insist that Islam is a religion of peace while threatening other people and then claiming that racism is OK in Islam. Has there ever been a peaceful but racist society anywhere in the world? Does this person realise which infamous figures he's keeping company with? He might as well have said 'I'm a totally nasty person and proud of it'.

So yes, last week was pretty groundbreaking when it came to getting rid of old taboos, even though they came from unexpected quarters. I suppose the old Malay pride in being well-mannered, soft-spoken and dignified is now dead and gone too, which is rather ironic considering that this undignified show of force was meant to uphold Malay 'dignity'.

The interesting thing is that all of this may be for nought. Before the red rally, a survey showed that a majority of Malays didn't support it. Last week's shenanigans probably converted no one to the cause. Few people were clear what it was about apart from some vague idea about protecting Malay dignity. I'm quite sure if someone in the middle of the crowd had started chanting 'Tolak GST' (Reject GST), the entire Padang Merbok would have joined in too. After all, they are the ones most affected by rising prices. Not much dignity if you have to cut back on essentials for your family.

Meanwhile more sensible Malaysians decided to celebrate Malaysia Day for what it really is: a day of togetherness and unity in diversity. Some of us had a picnic in KLCC park complete with balloons and cake for Malaysia's 52nd birthday. Total strangers dropped by and sat under the trees, made friends with one another and chatted about anything and everything. It was clear that we all had no problems with one another despite differences in background and that we all truly loved our country. We ended our picnic by singing the national anthem, something that was missing at Padang Merbok.

In another part of town, a whole day of festivities showcasing every culture in Malaysia was met with great enthusiasm. People tried different foods, watched cultural performances, witnessed a full Peranakan wedding, listened to music and basically spent time with one another in a warm togetherness. Our hearts burst with pride when Sean Ghazi sang a beautiful rendition of 'Tanah Pusaka', followed once again by the whole crowd singing 'NegaraKu'. Like midnight last August, everyone there owned the anthem, regardless of which Malaysian community they came from.

All of us were determined that Malaysia Day was a day of joy, fun and happiness and not one of anger and violence. We wanted our photos to be of people genuinely enjoying themselves and at peace with one another. We went home feeling good about ourselves. I don't know if the other crowd felt the same but I do hope that 'fun' would at least be one of words they would describe their event with.

One major difference between the red rally and previous yellow ones was easy to discern. If you don't mass-produce placards and banners and you make your own because you believe in a cause, the chances are you'll come up with some truly witty ones. Amidst anger about current issues, we could still laugh at such creativity. Instead of laughing at people.

*23 September 2015*

# Working Together to Find Cures and Solutions

When it comes to some issues, I sometimes wonder if they're too important to leave to politicians to handle.

There we were with smoggy skies and unbreathable air again. I repeat, again. After previous bad experiences and many promises by our leaders that they will do something about it, not only did the haze return, it was actually worse.

Did we learn anything from the last time? It started down south in our neighbouring country that was choked completely. You would think we would start wondering whether we would be hit next. Instead we twiddled our thumbs and watched as the haze made its way north, disrupting everything along the way. Could we not have foreseen this? And therefore could we not have done something quicker to at least mitigate it? Or issue warnings to those most vulnerable to be alert to the risks to their health? Before the 100% rise in asthma cases?

I don't know what it is about our country that we are so resistant to actually doing anything about prevention. No, I misstate that: we love preventive actions especially if they involve detention or the prevention of so-called immoralities. Mostly by methods for which there is no evidence of effectiveness.

But to do the actual hard work of studying and analysing an issue in order to find a fact-based implementable solution seems to be beyond us.

On Monday I sat in a plenary session at the 7th International

AIDS Society Conference on HIV Pathogenesis, Treatment and Prevention and listened to a doctor from Cambodia talking about their approach to managing the epidemic. He described the progression of their HIV programme as Cambodia 1.0, 2.0 and now 3.0 with a lot of analysis of their data. I truly don't know how accurate his analyses were but I was impressed at the issues they were striving to address including sensitive ones like sex work.

Although I have not been involved in HIV for seven years now, what seems obvious to me is that at most, we are at Malaysia 1.5 when it comes to HIV. That is because we are one of the few countries in the region to implement harm reduction programmes and to provide free antiretroviral treatment to Malaysians living with HIV. But that was a while ago and although that's something we should be proud of, we really have not moved on.

Trying to get updated statistics on HIV is difficult enough. But even more difficult is trying to get analyses of the statistics, or of other factors that contribute to the HIV epidemic, whether on the prevention or treatment side. I listened to a South African professor talk about the issues of transitioning care for children with HIV who grow into adults and had to wonder if anyone here was also thinking of the same.

The same is true of every government department, not just health. It would be interesting to know if the new Youth minister will commission studies to truly find out why some of our young men become *mat rempit*s, or get into drugs, or are so absent in our tertiary institutions. Or are those issues to be left to the police, or to Education? If there is anything new our current government can do to truly make a difference, it would be to recognise that many of these issues are cross-cutting and need the engagement and cooperation of several ministries working together and not in isolation.

Similarly, our Women's Ministry would do well to get someone to do a truly in-depth study of why child marriage or incest happen and what can be done to prevent these. Or why children keep drowning during the school holidays. Do we even really have facts on why so many babies get abandoned?

But we seem to have no appetite for knowing the real reasons why these issues arise in our society. Instead we would rather rely on speculation based often on someone's shallow knowledge or worse, prejudice. This is how we get ridiculous 'guidelines' on how to spot gay people, all of which seem to be based on a cheap telenovela somewhere.

If we are going to seriously right whatever is wrong in our society, we need to face them squarely. Today I heard a presentation on the dismal state of the Malayan tiger and it's obvious that the problem is human greed in all its forms. But unless we own up to that, then we can bid our tigers goodbye. How sad is that?

We need to hold up a mirror to ourselves and simply accept what we see. Then find realistic ways to make us be better so that we look better.

*13 July 2013*

# The Trouble with Silence

I read a curious piece of news the other day where one of our bigwigs said that by not criticising us, President Obama is actually supporting us with his silence.

I don't even know where to start with this apart from it making a good Monday morning laugh. As some people have pointed out, since when do we need the US's approval for anything? And secondly, when did we start reading people's minds that we know what they are thinking when they don't say anything? Could it be that we are simply number 1000 on Obama's list of priorities?

It just intrigued me, this line of thinking that silence means assent. You can extrapolate it to so many things. If our PM says nothing to cases of Bibles being confiscated or threatened with burning, does that mean he approves? When some people behave incredibly badly, making out that they are superior to other citizens and we hear nothing from our PM, does this mean he agrees with them? Or when he has absolutely nothing to say about the many abuses of the Sedition Act that are carried out, can we assume that it means he thinks there is nothing wrong with extending the jurisdiction of the Act way beyond what it is meant for?

This is the trouble with silence. Nobody really knows what it means. So we can only make up reasons, just as that bigwig is making for Obama. If I were the President of the United States, I'd swat that nonentity away for his presumption.

Maybe there is a culture of 'silence is assent' in our society. The best way to assure agreement in this way is by not telling anyone what trouble they are in. So that if they don't speak up, it must mean they don't have any objections. Hence, perhaps, why a state religious authority kept quiet about their fatwa that named Sisters in Islam as deviant. If we didn't find out before the three-month deadline, then surely we must agree to it! Ta da! Did they actually expect us to then go around introducing ourselves as 'Sesat in Selangor'? (Literally, 'Lost in Selangor'.)

Silence equals assent speaks volumes ironically about the lack of transparency in lawmaking in our religious institutions. Are laws made from whims and fancies of certain people? Should there not be more rigour in ensuring standards of justice are met before they can be passed? Should it not be so watertight that if it is met with so much negative feedback, the authorities can give their reasons why they passed it without much hesitation? Or what does silence mean in this case? Oops, maybe?

Malaysia is unique in the Muslim world in that fatwas can actually become law once gazetted. This means that if anyone contravenes them, you can be subject to some sort of punitive action. Which is why some fatwas, such as those against smoking or Amanah Saham, are not gazetted since it would mean an overwhelming number of people would have to be hauled off to jail. Someone must have thought that with this fatwa, only a small number of people would be punished so why not? Except that the fatwa itself is very wide since it covers 'organisations, individuals and institutions' that subscribe to 'liberalism and pluralism'. By that undefined measure, just about anybody who thinks differently can be caught by it. The courts will be kept very busy trying everyone, as if they didn't already have a backlog of divorces and child maintenance cases that they haven't dealt with yet.

If the message that differing opinions will not be tolerated is obtuse to some, there are plenty of young people who get it immediately. And they don't like it. We get letters and emails of support from so many young people who say that they can't take all this repression anymore. They have the brains to think for themselves, they say, to decide for themselves what they should or should not do in life. They want to learn more about their faith, but not in this sledgehammer style, through omission or silence, by simply not being allowed to talk about issues. Every day our religious authorities make themselves less and less relevant to our young by their condescending attitudes towards them.

In this case it would be a mistake to think that the silence of the young means they approve or they agree with all that our authorities do. If you look and listen carefully, they are speaking in many different ways, not necessarily in the bureaucratic way that our authorities normally do. Each attempt to clamp down on them only emboldens them more.

Perhaps if our leaders did some mind-reading, they'd see that the silence doesn't mean anything they thought it did.

*7 November 2014*

## Warriors Who Lack Vision

Imagine, if you will, a band of warriors making their way through some tall grass. They are armed to the teeth because they are convinced that within the dense foliage, there are untold numbers of hostile parties ready to attack them at any time.

As they make their way, not the least bit quietly, their nerves tense, they are on constant lookout for enemies. At the slightest sound or the faintest whiff of a possible attack, they pounce, with clubs and spears, and do their best to beat their presumed enemy to death. It's a take-no-prisoners approach, judge first before asking questions. Except that there is nobody to question once the warriors are done with them.

In this way, the warriors believe they are guarding the tall-grass territory that they live in. The 'enemy' is always unseen, they believe, so anything that seems different must be treated with suspicion at best, immediately 'dealt with' at worst. To do nothing is to allow these opponents to breed and their ideas to spread 'like a cancer'.

But the tall grass hides the true picture of what is happening because it hides the warriors' vision. They can only see what is at the sparse top of the grass and not what is underneath, where discontent is seething. The warriors cannot see that they are standing on the shoulders of those underneath and the glimpses and sounds of the 'enemies' they see and hear, and whom they attack immediately, are simply the attempts by those underneath to find air to breathe in the upper reaches of the grass.

In the undergrowth of the grass lie many humans hiding in the shadows fearful of the warriors. They work hard to keep the habitat growing, and for so long they have been quietly contributing to it as much as they can. But the warriors won't have it. The grass, they say, is only for the cleanest purest warriors, of which there are only a few. Those who do not fit into their definitions of 'clean' and 'pure' besmirch their habitat and therefore must either be gotten rid of or be rehabilitated to cleanse them of their 'impurities'.

The warrior class is a special one. To qualify, they have to be of a certain community and be male. The few females allowed to join can only do so if they agree with everything their male leaders say and do. All must agree never to use their brains, only their voices and it helps that they have many outlets at which their voices can be heard and listened to. Brawn is everything, might is always right, loud is proud.

The problem with being a warrior, however, is that one is required to have one's nerves perpetually on edge, beneath a paper-thin skin. One must be ready to see ghosts behind every door, crucifixes on every cookie, proselytisers under every carpet and porcine DNA in high-calorie junk food. Conviction of one's own rightness is a must, even when it is scientifically proven that one is wrong. Science is simply not the warrior's forte; therefore science is an unnecessary inconvenience.

Meanwhile, outside the land of the tall grass, where the grass is cut to a level where everyone can breathe the same air and all be seen and heard, people are progressing. Every day someone gets a chance in the sunlight to show an invention that makes life better for everyone, regardless of who they are. Innovators are rewarded and nobody pays attention to those who want to go back to the days of the tall grass.

But the warriors who live in the tall grass, because they cannot see beyond the grass they live in, do not fathom how far behind they are being left. Innovators who need air to breathe in order to be creative are trampled on, so eventually they escape the tall grass to live in lands where the grass is shorter. Anyone who complains of the unjust access to air is shot down immediately, and told that only those defending the right to keep the grass tall and dense are allowed to breathe.

Zoom out and looking at the globe from afar, we see that there are fewer and fewer patches of tall grass. Everywhere people are cutting the grass short to give everyone a chance in the sunshine, recognising that it is in everyone's nature to yearn for fresh air to breathe. With sunlight, everyone is happy and friendly with one another. The land of the short grass is calm and peaceful.

In the land of the tall grass, the warriors thrash wildly and fiercely at everything that moves, not realising that underneath there is in fact nothing.

*12 November 2014*

# Why Some Societies Collapse

I like to read odd books sometimes. In particular I like to read books about the human condition, not so much the philosophies behind it but as much as can be learnt from reality as possible.

One of the authors I really enjoy reading is Jared Diamond, an American academic best known for his books, *Guns, Germs and Steel*, *Collapse* and his latest, *The World Until Yesterday*. Diamond is known as a polymath, a person 'whose expertise spans a significant number of different subject areas; such a person is known to draw on complex bodies of knowledge to solve specific problems.' Prof. Diamond is an expert on physiology, biophysics, ornithology, environmentalism, history, ecology, geography, evolutionary ecology and anthropology. Today at age 76, he is professor of geography at the University of California Los Angeles.

Reading any of Prof. Diamond's books really makes you understand the world in a different way because of his ability to weave together different threads of knowledge. For instance, in his book *Collapse*, which discusses why some societies collapse while others are resilient, he points out that what we think of as political and social problems arise out of some very basic issues of survival. In the case of Rwanda, famously depicted as a civil war between the Hutu and the Tutsi, at its most basic, it was about the tensions that arise when people are so squeezed together that the amount of land they have to grow food on is too small to be productive.

Similarly in *The World Until Yesterday*, which compares traditional hunter-gatherer societies with state societies (i.e. the 'developed' world), when people are asked why they go to war with each other, the answers are usually simple things like 'revenge', 'women' or 'pigs' or 'cattle'. But at heart it is about ensuring the survival of the society you live in, no matter what the size. He backs up all these assertions with the many anthropological, archaeological and historical studies that have been done about societies around the world and shows that we cannot really judge them all by the same values.

For instance we may think that tribal societies in places like Papua New Guinea or parts of Africa are 'backward' but that is because we are judging them by our standards. Indeed there is much to admire in their attitudes towards children and in the way they resolve disputes. On the other hand, there is much about 'modern' society today which these tribal people would find appalling, especially in the way we sometimes treat our old people.

This is not to say that everything about these tribal hunter-gatherer communities is wonderful. Until relatively recently, many of them lived in a constant state of warfare and things like infanticide was very common, for the most practical reasons. Most of us would not want to give up the benefits of living in a settled centralised state for such nomadic hand-to-mouth lifestyles. But there are some things which we do which are not that far off from those 'primitive' habits.

Prof. Diamond compares only Western lifestyles with the tribal communities he did field studies on. Which means that the contrasts can be big. If he had studied Asian soceities however, he would have found us somewhere in the middle. For instance, the Asian extended family and the way our children are cared for by many adults, not just their parents, is more akin to the way hunter-gatherer communities in Papua New Guinea or the Amazon live. The way we coddle our children too is more similar to those communities than to that of Western parenting which stresses independence.

Yet children from these hunter-gatherer communities are observed to become very confident adults who are well-versed in many adult responsibilities such as foraging for food, caring for children and protecting their communities. While children brought up in the Western style often grow up very protected but then unable to take on adult responsibilities when they come of age. For instance, we disapprove of early marriage because our children are often unprepared to be parents even after being biologically ready. But children in tribal communities, who have not only been observing their parents daily but also have had to help care for younger siblings, know exactly what to do should they have children even at very young ages.

What is confusing for us Malaysians is that we are very much a society in transition, not quite a society living hand-to-mouth but not quite yet a modern one, despite our buildings and gadgets. Our attitudes towards many things hark back to a different type of society where everyone knew each other and relationships were set in certain ways. But things have changed very rapidly for us.

We should therefore take heed of Prof. Diamond's main discovery in *Collapse*: if as a society we do not adapt fast enough to change, we will face collapse.

*28 August 2014*

# Simple Guide to Success in Malaysia

As everyone in this country is an expert in giving advice to everyone else, I thought I would join in and give generously of my totally unsolicited counsel to all those aspiring to join cupboards or closets of any kind. Any likenesses to anything familiar around us is, naturally, completely a coincidence.

First of all, please get it out of your head that you are wanted or needed because you have expertise of any kind. Who cares if you have a double degree in How to Make Anything Good and How to Make Anything Better? What you need is a Ph.D in How To Make Your Boss Feel Good, with a minor on How To Make Your Boss Look Really Good. It would also help if you have expertise in How To Clean Up Messes, especially if it involves getting rid of Messy People.

Secondly, you have to audition for the job. Don't ever expect to be picked out of obscurity like some Cinderella. Let's not forget that Cinders didn't really get an invitation to the Ball, but her ugly stepsisters did. And they worked for it damn hard by making sure they got noticed. So find a way to get attention, never mind if it means making a spectacle of yourself. Who cares if you look and sound like a fool as long as your potential boss likes it? The path to position and lucre is strewn with puffery and pomp! Pledge loyalty even if nobody asked you to! That counts as double points.

Thirdly, always be humble and say you had not expected this at all but it must have been divine intervention. Who in their right mind would question what the Almighty wants? And He must have spoken through his vessel, your soon-to-be Boss. George W. Bush said God made him president to do His will on earth. Surely if an American can claim that, we can too!

Fourthly, don't be picky about what you are given. Just be grateful! What does it matter anyway? They all come with nice perks like a nice house (there must be a renovation budget), nice car with driver, first-class travel for you and the Mrs, and all sorts of other things you've only heard about from others but can now experience first-hand. So what if the work is crushingly dull? Someone else can read all those papers for you and give you a summary. And oops, if you miss a few things in there, there are lots of people you can blame, even despatch clerks. Why worry, you've hit the big time!

Fifthly, now that you've got it, your job is to smile and nod your head. Vigorously. All the time. Get yourself photographed with the boss as much as possible, preferably looking at him with utter adoration. If you can hold up a suitable adoring placard, better still. Though some have found that this is no insurance for job security. Maybe practise hand-kissing as an alternative.

Sixthly, let's not forget that you are a package deal which your spouse is a part of. Train her well because her job is as important as yours. Quite the opposite from you, her job is not to compete with her boss. So make sure that if you want to buy pretty expensive things for her (and now you can!), don't let her wear them in front of her boss. Especially if she looks quite hot in them. Support local brands and dress your other half in them. Leave the international imports to her boss and coach her in the right admiring phrases to murmur.

Seventhly, seen the TV series, 'Entourage'? That's what you need, an entourage. Surround yourself with all sorts of folks who can be given menial jobs dressed up as important by putting them in the right clothes. No big man is without his entourage, to carry bags, carry shopping, check you in at airports, that sort of thing. Never ever have to do a single thing yourself again.

Eighthly, be part of an entourage yourself. It is highly important that you keep yourself within your boss's line of sight at all times, because you don't want him to forget you exist. Or to overlook you the next time he wants to clear out his cupboard. So follow him everywhere; after all that is your main job. It's also your spouse's job to be a handmaiden in her boss's entourage so if she gets called upon to serve, give her your blessing. It will be rewarding.

There you have it, eight tips on how to succeed in life in our dear country. The folks out there who have to actually work to survive each day wish you lots of luck. Drop some crumbs some time.

*30 July 2015*

# THE LISTS

# Hopes for New Leaders

Well, the changeover went smoothly didn't it*? Just a simple and dignified ceremony and that was it. We should be proud that it could be so simple. I was just grateful to be invited to the ceremony since 22 years ago, nobody remembered to invite family members along.

But life goes on and we all pin hopes on new leaders that they will put right what was not done before. I'm also one of those with a wish list that I hope someone somewhere will take into consideration. Here goes:

1.  I hope we can put an end to denial and complacency when it comes to social problems such as drugs, violence against women and HIV/AIDS. Too often we see statistics blithely being quoted with no explanation except for a cursory statement about things being 'under control'. (It would help if those asking questions in Parliament, for instance, were a bit more difficult to satisfy with just numbers.). The truth is this: we have a bigger drug problem than we did 20 years ago with no solution in sight. The only response we ever get is the same old thing over and over again which we know hasn't worked. In addition, we have an HIV/AIDS problem which is nowhere near under control and which is now reaching out to the general public. But then, when you have some people in authority who see

AIDS as the 'final solution' to the drug problem, is it any wonder that little realistic effort is being made to control the epidemic?

2. Violence against women is no small matter either. Everyday we read in the papers about women being molested, abused, raped, kidnapped and even murdered. Why are we still complacent about this? Is it because we don't value our women enough? Violence against women is a blight on our society and we should be collectively ashamed that it happens. We shouldn't be spending time splitting hairs about whether it happens at home or in public, between married people or not. If a man abuses or kills his wife, it doesn't make him any better than a man who kills a stranger. That marriage licence enjoins him to love and respect his wife, not abuse her.

3. I read with horror a report that someone had described the Malaysian HIV/AIDS epidemic as under control. How can this be when, compared to Australia which has roughly the same population, we have about four times more cases than they do? Last year, they had 800 new cases and we had almost 7000. And still we think that AIDS is the result of 'Westernised' behaviour? Please, let us get real!

4. Last week the Censor Board banned some books because they may affect us mentally and make us believe in mystical things. As if we don't already! We make all these

tenuous leaps between cause and effect that sometimes I think it is a way of avoiding the truth about why we behave a certain way. Some of my favourites are 'smoking makes you take drugs' and 'drinking soya bean makes you gay'. It is very likely that all drug users smoke, but not all smokers take drugs. Otherwise, what about all those doctors, executives, religious officials and politicians who smoke? Are they all potential drug users? As for the soya bean connection ... well, we should educate all those *mat salleh* mothers in San Francisco and Sydney about the dangers of tofu.

5.  Talking about the Censor Board, the dismantling of this is certainly high on my wish list. We cannot keep on a censorship mentality that is stuck in 1952 and sees subversive elements behind every page and pixel. How do we become a k-economy when some people insist on controlling the k that we get? If knowledge is power, then the control of knowledge is even greater power. Right now it is in the hands of some retired civil servants who believe we will all be influenced by just seeing an image, reading or hearing a word. This is probably why we have not developed into a literate thinking society. And it's almost 2004!

6.  Let us respect our young people more. We talk about respecting our elders all the time. That's fine but we need to also respect our young as people with vast potential, ideas, capabilities, talent to bring our country to the

fore even more. Yet every day we see our young being put down for being immature and immoral, forced into compartments and categories that don't suit them, rarely consulted on programmes we assume will be good for them. We spend so much time trying to mould them into our own images, assuming all this time that our images are perfect. We don't give them space to breathe, think and show what they can do. We don't even realise that underneath they are simmering and looking for outlets where they can be themselves and express themselves. We only let them express themselves in approved ways. It's a question of control. We have to accept that we can't really control what happens in 20 years' time. All we can do is provide a basic foundation and then let the next generations do what they think is best, even if it's not what we think is best. We have to let our baby birds fly.

Once I get started on a wish list, it can go on and on. So I'll just stop with these few things first. Not too much to ask, is it?

*12 November 003*

* Prime Minister Dato' Seri Dr Mahathir Mohamad retired from the premiership after 22 years and officially handed over to Dato' Seri Abdullah Ahmad Badawi on 31 October 2003.

# Things to be Grateful For

It's the end of the year finally. Just by the sheer exhaustion I feel I can't say that this has been the best year ever. This year we had war and SARS, which cast a cloud over just about everything, and somehow made even things on a more individual and personal level seem gloomy. I think of myself as a general optimist but when you feel so tired, it's a bit hard to do.

Writing this column this year has proven to be a bigger test in discipline than usual. My patient editors have tolerated me being late handing in my pieces, sometimes missing them altogether, with more generosity that I can reasonably expect. This year I tried to expand my writing responsibilities by doing some writing for books and wound up with an overloaded schedule that is still being cleared even now. It should teach me not to be too ambitious and also to say no more forcefully. (I say that with great optimism although everyone knows I have the worst record for turning down anything.)

Despite a year that's been far from exemplary, I prefer to see the silver linings among the grey clouds. Here are some of the things I have been grateful for:

1.  An era passed and we have a new prime minister, with a little pomp, a lot of smiles and much hope. We should all take credit for that.

2. Peace became fashionable, even though it is still non-existent. Once upon a time, peace seemed to be confined to happy hippies. Now most of the world has realised that it cannot be taken for granted and it must be worked on. And that peace cannot be separated from human rights. If you believe that, on a macro level, people have a right to govern themselves and make their own decisions about their future, then we must also practise it at a micro level. The only way we can have peace between countries is when we have peace at community and individual levels. When we respect the right of individuals to be who they are, as long as they do not hurt anyone else. We have to stop assuming that people are essentially bad and carry out pre-emptive strikes on them by enacting laws that govern personal behaviours, invade privacy and stamp on their rights. Wanting to stop people from withdrawing their EPF savings at age 55 because they might just fritter it all away is a fine example of not respecting people's ability to think for themselves and tarring everyone with the same brush. Why don't we try tarring everyone with a positive brush for a change? If we don't stop these types of pre-emptive strikes on individuals, how can we complain about governments wanting to carry out pre-emptive strikes against other countries? The logic is the same after all.

3. The supreme irony that the so-called 'Leader of the Free World' is the least free person on earth today. Thanks to his incredibly unenlightened policies, President George

W. Bush can hardly go to the toilet without a bomb squad preceding him. I was in New York City when half the city was blocked off just because he was going to speak at the United Nations. I wonder sometimes whether, at bedtime, he ever puts two and two together and realises that the reason why he can't run out to the local 7-11 to get a carton of milk is because there are any number of people who hate him enough to want to do some injury to him. What sort of life is that? There is something weird about the fact that all former presidents of the United States get to have Secret Service protection for the rest of their lives after retirement. What are they being protected from? People's long memories? The weirdest thing of all is that, more often than not, the biggest threats come from their own people and people they think of as friends. Bush has not travelled much since he became president but even when he travels to a country he thinks of as friendly (well, he has one friend there), he needs to put on almost armour-plated defense lines everywhere. President Aznar of Spain is probably praying that his pal George never wants to come visit.

4. We should therefore be grateful that, despite not being part of the 'free' world, we can still go up to the PM and shake his hand during Hari Raya open house without first being frisked. And the only thing he has to worry about when he wants to go to the supermarket to get his favourite can of sardines is the number of people who want to take photos with him.

5. Michael Moore. Never mind that he looks a mess, his mind and heart aren't. Through his books and films, he makes you believe that not all Americans are like Bush, Cheney, Rumsfeld and Rice. He may sound like he's ranting but he backs up everything with facts and figures that can only make you gasp with awe. Take his most recent posting about the fake turkey that Bush 'carved' on his Thanksgiving trip to his troops in Iraq. Fact is definitely stranger than fiction, and as Moore likes to say, this is a fictitious government in the US. In 2004, I wish the American people all the best in bringing in a real government, one with more heart and more brains.

6. On a smaller scale, I am grateful for Malaysians. We're not perfect, we can be completely awful, especially on the roads, but we're us. We like our food, we like shopping, we like putting in our two-sen worth about everything. We're generally nice to one another, although we don't always notice when we aren't. (To the parents of the kids who hogged the little carousel at the MegaMall yesterday, there are other little kids in the world too, you know!). I may not be the best judge since people are mostly nice to me (with some truly rotten exceptions) but then why shouldn't I be grateful for that? I like to believe in the best of people, even when I have met some dreadful ones. One of the worst people I know once inspired me by a speech he made about compassion. Either I was easily taken in, or he changed. I still learnt something about compassion from him and that's not to be forgotten.

Lastly, we should remember that everything we have did not come by accident. We worked for it and we should really travel more to truly understand that. Just as we keep saying we should not emulate the West, we should also look carefully at whom we do want to emulate. People want to emulate us not because we are so strict and have such supposedly Asian (i.e. better) values. It is because, with our economic development, we are considered free people, free from hunger, poverty, disease and oppression. It's a freedom not to be taken for granted however and we should fight to maintain our status as leaders of the aspiring free world. Now that would turn the world on its head, wouldn't it?

Happy New Year!

*24 December 2003*

# Collective Resolutions

It's that time of year again and it looks like every columnist (and letter writer) is putting in a wish list for the new year. So as not to be left out, I'll do the same.

I'm not going to do a list of personal resolutions because none of them are going to have much bearing on our society and country (unless me learning to cook is really of earth-shaking significance). So I'd like to do a list of collective resolutions that we all should make together. Here goes:

1. Let's decide to bring back ethics. According to my dictionary, that means a system of moral principles governing the appropriate conduct for an individual or group. So it means that we all undertake not to lie, cheat or steal. That includes people in public office of course. In fact, let's demand better ethics from people in public office. When they've done something wrong, they do the ethical thing by owning up, apologising and maybe even resigning. Let's also insist that saying terrible, unsubstantiated things about people is not news, it's unethical.

2. Let's call a spade a spade. If someone in public office says something stupid, as they are often wont to do, let's just tell them they are stupid. Let's not beat about the bush

so that their feelings won't be hurt. Hey, when they say dumb things, I feel hurt because they think I'm mentally deficient. Why is it that they are allowed to insult us and we are just supposed to swallow it? Getting a high post doesn't make you an intellectual giant so let's call a midget a midget when we need to.

3. Let's really celebrate diversity in all its forms. I said celebrate, not just acknowledge. I think I am rich because I have friends of different races, religions, nationalities, socio-economic status, political and sexual orientation. I love that about my life, it's what makes it interesting. We should all take a look at our lives and see if we can truly celebrate its diversity. Not just give a cursory nod to it.

4. Let's get literate, not literal. Let's try and understand irony, nuance and different shades of meaning. Let's not insist that everything has to hit us between the eyes before we understand it. Let's just grow up.

5. Let us get militant about getting good service. Let us no longer tolerate people who keep you on hold on the phone and never come back, sales assistants who don't know what they are selling, people who don't keep promises, people who blow you off if you ask too many questions. It's become so bad that the other day when I asked a question at an information counter and the person manning it could actually answer, I was so shocked. Good service must become the norm, not the exception.

6. Let us not tolerate people who break traffic rules. And let us insist that there are police to enforce those rules. Why does everyone stop on yellow boxes, park on double lines, beat red lights, keep driving when people are using zebra crossings these days? We had to know these rules when we took our driving tests. Are we supposed to ignore them once we've got our licences?

7. Let us refuse to be condescended to by bureaucrats. If they try and tell us we are unpatriotic just because we ask difficult questions, let us tell them where to go. We are paying their salaries, allowances, first-class tickets with our taxes after all. And please, let us insist on knowing why they waste our money.

8. Let us not endure mediocrity in anything we do. If something is not really good, let's not say it's good 'by Malaysian standards' unless we mean that our standards are really low. We should promote only the best, not the second or third best. We should benchmark ourselves against the best in the world and, if we fall short, then aim higher and work harder. We should never be content to be 'jaguh kampung' (local hero) or the one-eyed king among the blind.

9. Let us stop being feudal and automatically bow and scrape to those with titles. It's so amazing who gets titles these days that you start feeling, like Groucho Marx, that it's becoming a club you don't want to be a member of.

10. Let us stop finding excuses for not doing the right thing. If something difficult needs to be done, let's stop fidgeting, hemming and hawing and then not do it. Or better still, let's hold the hemmers and hawers responsible for the disasters they cause. The rule of thumb should be that if something eases the suffering of people, it's the right thing.

11. Let us really listen to other people, especially when they are saying things we don't like to hear. Just because we don't like it doesn't mean it's not true. And let us ask them questions because we really want to know, not because we want an opportunity to attack or to pontificate.

It's funny how easy it was to do a list. In fact if it weren't for my word limit, I could probably find a lot more to add. But I won't, because if we can do even half of this, I would be happy. That's not accepting mediocrity, it's understanding reality.

Happy New Year everyone!

*29 December 2004*

# Clarification Needed

I know many people start the New Year fresh but I am starting it feeling a bit befuddled. Not because I partied so hard on New Year's Eve but because I left last year quite confused by many things. It would really be good if someone could clarify some of these:

1. I still don't get why we let Parliament pass a law that was flawed. And how come one minister claims that she had many objections to it, while another minister claimed that it was 'perfect'? And how come, considering that it's shredded the government's reputation domestically and internationally, it wasn't discussed at the first Cabinet meeting of the year?

2. What is Black Metal? Do these kids really worship Satan or are these just symbols meant to annoy parents and other adults in authority? How much more dangerous to society are these kids compared to men who commit incest with their daughters, say? Are they more dangerous than secret societies with three line logos that recruit young boys to commit crime?

3. How come men only accuse women of being emotional when they don't agree with them, but never when they

agree with them? It seems to me that the minute we start debating polygamy, men can get very emotional themselves, start stamping their feet and unashamedly declare that they might be forced to commit sin. I think we should just let them lah.

4. Ours is a country where, as long as it's legal, sex is very much encouraged. This is not the same as encouraging family values, because these can really only be nurtured if you have one family, not two, three or four. Actually when you consider that the ruling is four at a time, and not four in your entire lifetime, there could well be many more than four families being brought up with no values. How does this gel with all our 'pembangunan keluarga' (family development)? Does this mean we have to *bangun* (develop) as many families from one man as possible?

5. Why is it that we don't get outraged when we hear stories from other countries about men who kill their young daughters simply because they had a boyfriend? Considering that they are always kindred spirits in faith, don't we feel ashamed? Or is our silence just a manifestation of that shame?

6. When are we going to get to the stage where people take credit for the things they actually worked for, and not for what others did? Do we not believe that hard work equals results anymore? How can we tell our kids they need to work hard, when adults don't?

7. Can't we have basic IQ tests for MPs? How about one standard test for when they become MPs, and then an even higher one if they get made ministers? I shudder at the thought of any of them meeting any foreigners! I'd just like to go through a year without having to feel embarrassed.

8. We love drawing stereotypes about the West, about how permissive and immoral they are. What we don't realise is that they have stereotypes about us too, assuming we are backward intellectually, socially, economically, politically. This annoys us, and then we go on and prove them right... by being backward intellectually if nothing else. We think it really proves our intellectual superiority when we say that we cannot talk about something because it's too sensitive.

9. We want our young people to become leaders of our country. So to do that, we quash them into bland moulds, narrow their breathing space until they choke, keep telling them they are essentially bad, and then expect them to do a good job. Some leaders they are going to make.

I could go on, but starting the year with these things I'm confused about seems more than enough for anyone. Here's to a year of clearmindedness and clarity!

*12 January 2006*

# Suggested Rules for Men

Ho hum, here we go again. Is there no end to this ceaseless blaming of all forms of evil on women, just because they may not want to cover their heads? But I am really heartened by the many sensible retorts by various people, mostly ordinary citizens, who rightly pointed out that we really should get past the habit of blaming women for the bad things that happens to them, and letting perpetrators get away.

I'm sure that the Majlis Perbandaran Kota Baru (Kota Baru Municipal Council, MPKB) values all of its citizens and doesn't really intend to discriminate just against women, no matter how natural the impulse might be. I'm sure given half the chance, besides dreaming up more and more rules for women, those MPKB wise men can also come up with rules for their male denizens just to show that they can be fair.

Here, therefore, are some rules I would suggest that the MPKB (and in fact all other local authorities) implement for men:

1. Men who do not use deodorant will be fined RM500. Body odour can cause offence to other people, of both sexes. Furthermore, some people find the musky, sweaty fragrance that some men give off quite, um, arousing. Therefore this can considered a hazard to public morality. Hence, stiff fines should be imposed to prevent any untoward incidents. Perhaps a deodorant company can

be roped in to sponsor a campaign for the prevention of offensive odours.

2.  Men who do not have clean fingernails will be fined RM500. Our religion exhorts us to always keep ourselves clean. Hands should always be washed especially before eating. Hence, it stands to reason that blackened fingernails imply a clear distance between soap and hands. Perhaps the MPKB could hand out free nail brushes and have classes on how to use them. No woman should be expected to handle anything that has been touched by any male with dirty fingernails.

3.  Men must dress decently or be fined a minimum of RM500. Decently means clean clothes, pants that are not about to drop off and shoes, not slippers. We might even consider unmatched clothes and dirty sarongs as indecent. And, oh yes, the Visible Panty Line rule should extend to those who insist on wearing white robes too.

4.  Men who look at women up and down, up and down, regardless of how the women are dressed should be fined RM10,000 or 10 strokes of the cane. This should apply to any man, regardless of race, religion or rank, as the Qur'an clearly exhorts men to 'lower their gaze'. Extra fines and extra strokes should also be imposed for those who, besides leering, also make weird noises and, um, ungentlemanly remarks. No exemptions will be given for remarks made in Arabic.

5. Men with greasy hair, overlong nose and ear hairs and unkempt beards will be reprimanded for being aesthetically offensive. Perhaps a campaign sponsored by shampoo and shaving cream companies might be useful. Overlong untrimmed beards may harbour all manner of cooties, and are therefore just as unhygienic as dirty fingernails (sometimes all of these are found on the same person). Therefore these types of men can be deemed public health hazards. Women should be allowed to carry disinfecting sprays to protect themselves from such dangers.

6. Men may not wear makeup, such as black eyeliner, and overbearing fragrances, especially those meant to cover the pungence of unwashed bodies. Only the smell of soap will be tolerated.

I'm sure the MPKB really can't argue with these simple rules. Wouldn't it be nice if they set the example for all the other towns and cities in Malaysia if they could boast the cleanest and best-smelling men in the country?

While we are on the subject of dress, I want to congratulate that Bahraini woman who won the 200-metre gold medal at the Asian Games. It just goes to show that women can do anything, if they put their heart and soul into it. But before anyone gets too excited about how wearing the hijab somehow contributed to her medal, let us not forget the training that she obviously put in, not to mention the sheer dedication and commitment to her sport that would also have been required. If all it takes is a hijab to win races, then we should get all the men to cover up as well and see how they do.

And let me nominate for the Breath of Fresh Air Award, the new mufti of Perlis, for his courage in saying the right thing, and in restoring our faith in the justice and equality inherent in Islam. May he always stand his ground, and be the vanguard of change that we so badly need.

I wish everybody a Happy 2007!

*20 December 2006*

# Resolutions Others Should Make

There's something about the first day of a new year that is akin to a particular addiction of mine, a new notebook. I collect notebooks just to savour their clean empty pages as if they promise wonders that can't be sullied by merely writing them down. By keeping them empty, they hold more hope than if I covered their pages with my scratchy handwriting. It's not an environmentally correct obsession to be sure but there you are.

A new year often feels like a fresh start even while we can't avoid bringing along the baggage from the previous year. It's a border checkpoint where we need to pause and examine our papers to ensure that we have the right credentials to carry on our journey. If in the previous year we've been angry and tempestuous, it is time to calm down and coolly look at the road ahead. If, instead, we've been complacent, it may be time to look up and survey the landscape to see whether we truly like it the way it is.

Traditionally people make resolutions at the beginning of a new year, to start a diet, to learn something new, to be nicer to others. Most of these they won't keep. But at least making a resolution signals the intention to change and do something good for oneself or for others. I'm not much different when it comes to making resolutions. I try not to make any I can't keep, going on a diet being on top of the list. At the most, I am resolving to be nicer to others and to say thank you more.

Of course it's tempting to do my annual list of resolutions that

I wish other people would make. They will never keep them either but still, one can hope. So here goes (apologies for any repeats from last year, especially the resolutions for politicians):

1.  Politicians should resolve to count to ten before they say anything, no matter how trivial. In fact, the more trivial the issue, the more they should count to 100 preferably.

2.  If they have to say anything at all, politicians should resolve to judge what they are about to say by this criterion: will this statement make me look intelligent or like a fool? Preferably they should ask someone else to assess the statement on the assumption that, generally, they themselves cannot tell the difference between an intelligent and a foolish statement.

3.  Malaysians should resolve to understand that they no longer live in a village where outsiders have no business poking their noses in. Outsiders can now not only pretty much look into your underwear drawer, they can even comment on the state of your underwear. By the same token, if we want to, we can also look into other people's dirty linen baskets AND comment on them. Just because we choose not to, does not mean that others are also obliged to choose not to comment on ours.

4.  It would be nice for our people to resolve to understand that democracy is not something that happens once every five years but is something we should live and breathe

every day. It is our right to say something when we are unhappy, even if it is only a few of us that are unhappy. Nobody should consider themselves 100 percent satisfied when their fellow citizens are not. It is better for everybody to be 90 percent happy than to have some who are fully satisfied and others who are extremely discontented.

5. Following which, we should all resolve to acknowledge that gaps exist that need to be filled. Everybody needs to understand each other, not just some. In fact, it is incumbent on the majority to do more to understand and respect the minority.

6. Let us resolve to stop blaming others for our own shortcomings. We all have our part to play and we should play them well. It is not the fault of victims when criminals are not caught nor of teachers when kids go awry. We also need to recognise that systemic failures create an environment where nobody gets to do their job well. Righting the system is the first step.

Lastly, we need to redefine patriots as people who care about their country regardless of whether they toe the line or not. If we choose to live here we have a stake in it and we have a right to express our concerns in any way we feel they will be heard. It is sometimes those who are deaf who are the lesser patriots.

May we all have an enlightened 2008!

*2 January 2008*

# Suggestions for the Government

With the recent hike in fuel prices and the Government's exhortations for us to change our lifestyles in order to cope, may I provide here some suggestions for the Government and those who work for it to 'share our burden'.

1. Stop having meetings, especially out at resorts far enough away to be able to claim transport allowances. Have online meetings instead or teleconferences. Use Skype or chat.

2. No need to order special pens, bags, T-shirts, notepads and other goodies for those same meetings.

3. No need to order *kuih* for mid-morning or teatime meetings in Government offices, or *nasi biryani* lunches for those meetings that happen to end just at lunchtime.

4. Cancel all trips for Government servants to conferences overseas unless they return with full reports of what they did there, who they met and what they learnt and how they mean to apply what they learnt at home. Ask them to do presentations to colleagues who did not get to go on the most interesting and important papers that they read.

5. Scrutinise invoices for contracts to make sure they are

truly reflective of what those projects or supplies cost.

6.  Stop elaborate launches for Government programmes. In particular, stop the buying of souvenirs, special batik shirts, corsages, bouquets and caps.

7.  Make all civil servants and politicians travel economy class. That means really travelling at the back of the plane and not buying full-fare economy class tickets that allow them to be upgraded to business class.

8.  Stop having the full complement of police escorts, to cut down on petrol costs. If they need to be somewhere by a certain time, start earlier like the rest of us. Wouldn't be a bad thing for them to also experience a traffic jam.

9.  Once a week (or more), have ministers use public transport so they know what everyone else has to suffer. This might provide them with the incentive to improve them.

10. Once a week, let ministers go to a market to buy food for their families with instructions not to spend more than RM100.

11. Get ministers to carpool. They might get more work done just by being able to talk to each other to see what could be coordinated between their ministries. For instance, the ministers of Health and Women could discuss what to do about women's health issues in the car on the way to work.

Maybe have a secretary to travel in the front seat to take down notes on what was discussed. By the time they get to their offices, things can get implemented.

12. Once a month, get civil servants to work with one disadvantaged group in order to be better able to appreciate their problems. It could be blind people one month, hearing-disabled people the next, Orang Asli the following month and People Living with HIV/AIDS after that. We could start buddy systems which pair one civil servant with one disadvantaged person and at the end of it, ask each pair to make recommendations on how to make life better for each other. This might get rid of the problem of desk jockeys, people who never stray very far from their desks yet make policies for people they know nothing about.

13. Have PA systems that shout out the name of the officers who have to serve people at government officers so that people get the services they came for and don't have to keep coming back just because the officer is out having coffee. No counter should be left unmanned for more than five minutes before the officer is paged to go back to their stations. This should cut down waiting time for the public and saves them transport costs in having to keep returning just to get one thing done.

14. Government officers who lose people's files should be fined and have their names publicised for being careless

and causing inconvenience to the public. Instead of making the public travel to their offices several times to deal with their problems, they should travel to go see their client and deal with it right there and then. And every officer who goes out of the office should be given a reasonable time to get his work done after which they are expected back in their office so they don't waste time doing something else.

15. And newspapers should save paper by reporting real news rather than the non-news that they carry, particularly nonsensical utterances by politicians.

As they say, we need to do this all together in order to make a difference. So if the Government and politicians make these lifestyle changes, I will do my part and change mine.

*18 June 2008*

# 'Can Do' Fatwas

It's been a long time since I've made my lists so in keeping with recent issues I thought I would make a list of fatwas I'd like see.

Now, some people think that I have something against fatwas. Actually I think they can be helpful in providing guidance to Muslims on how to conduct their lives. I do have issues with fatwas that deal only with petty things while ignoring much more important things in life. What's more, most fatwas seem to be only about what you cannot do, rather than what you can.

Having seen how the National Fatwa Council will respond to individual complaints and suggestions for fatwas, I thought I would come up with a list of 'Can Do' fatwas it should consider issuing. None of them will attract punishment if not adhered to, at least not in this world. But I think they would go a long way towards making Muslims, and even non-Muslims, better people. So here goes.

We should have fatwas that:

1.  Tell people that the only way to make money is to work hard. No get-rich-schemes that promise you can earn thousands in a week, no pyramid plans, no going to bomohs, no cosying up to the influential and certainly no bribery and corruption.

2. Say that women can be leaders in any field or workplace, as long as they treat those they lead with equality and fairness. And those men who have problems with women being leaders are forgetting that the Prophet (pbuh) used to work for his wife Khatijah, and that everyone considered his daughter Aishah a respected leader in her community.

3. Emphasise that the best men are those who never neglect their wives and children, even when they are no longer married to them. Therefore men who abscond from their duties are not to be excused or celebrated in any way.

4. Say that the best parents are those who stay home and read with their children and help them with their homework every school night.

5. Emphasise that the best Muslims are those who read the Qur'an and work to understand it themselves.

6. Say that discriminatory attitudes towards people different from ourselves are not allowed in Islam.

7. Outline ways in which we should show consideration for one another, such as by keeping public toilets clean, not throwing rubbish everywhere and not parking indiscriminately so that other people are inconvenienced.

8. Point out that envy and jealousy are the worst traits anyone

could have, especially when other people are successful. The good Muslim should be happy for others when they are successful and not begrudge them or cast aspersions on their abilities.

9. Encourage charity to be active and not passive. Charity means actually devoting time and effort to doing something to help others and not merely writing cheques. Charity also means helping those truly in need and not just to get attention.

10. Underscore that a good Muslim is one that is polite and well-mannered, and should never curse, swear and act in an offensive manner to others, especially women, the disabled and people from other communities. This is not least because such bad manners reflect poorly on one's upbringing and are therefore disrespectful to one's own parents.

11. Take to task judges in any court who are biased towards anyone based on sex, race, religion or creed.

12. Declare fatwas and laws that are unjust as null and void.

13. Encourage people to be happy by doing what makes them happy, such as by making music, creating art or playing sport, as long as they don't harm anyone else. And if these things offend anyone, they have to say clearly why they are offended so that they do not spoil everyone else's fun.

14. Remind people that nature is a gift from God and should not be taken for granted, nor disrespected and exploited. Disasters are not to be blamed on God when there are perfectly human explanations for them. Keeping our rivers, forests and air clean is the duty of each of us, not of someone else.

15. Emphasise that learning and being knowledgeable is also a duty because it helps us to be better people and citizens. Furthermore, we should learn from far and wide and especially learn science and technology.

16. Encourage people to deal with real-life problems with contemporary solutions and not pretend they don't exist, or deal with them through unjust solutions or hocus-pocus.

17. Assures people that life is not a booby trap where you spend all your time trying to avoid small mistakes out of fear of major retribution. God is Ever Merciful and Compassionate and understands that you're only human.

That's my fatwa wish list for 2009. May at least some come true!

*17 December 2008*

# The Good, The Bad and The New Year

Since this is my last column for the year, I thought I'd do my usual list exercise. It has been a very eventful year to say the least so I thought I would list out what I've been happy about and what I haven't been happy about this year.

Let's start off with Things I Wasn't Happy About:

1.  The way some people behave so badly with such impunity, as if they know they can do anything and get away with it. Top of the list are those 'cowhead protestors' and their brethren who declared Malays 'first-class citizens' and all others, 'second-class citizens'. No throwing the book of sedition at them, not even a sharp rap on the knuckles?

2.  The shrinking of public space for debate and discussion especially on matters of religion and race. If anyone tries to give alternative viewpoints, they are immediately shouted down or a police report is made charging them with everything from insulting God, religion, the Sultan and whoever has the thinnest skin. And we call ourselves a modern nation?

3.  The refusal to get out from under the cloak of denial on all social problems. If there is a problem among our people,

the answer is always more religion, particularly the form that refuses to entertain any discussion on the subject. Somehow we expect the matter to disappear just like that. Unfortunately they fester and will ooze slime endlessly whether we like it or not. This would include issues like drug use, *mat rempit* and incest.

4.  Related to that is the apparent wish that the Kartika* problem would just go away. It is clear now that nobody really wants to whip her. But unless someone clearly states that she's been pardoned, her life will remain in suspension. There is nothing just and fair about leaving her in abeyance like that. Some closure for her is needed.

5.  In conjunction with that is the apparent belief that the only good Muslim is the one that wants to be punished while those who question injustice are painted as disbelievers. At the same time, those who are disobeying the courts, such as the men who are refusing to pay court-ordered maintenance for their children, are never painted as bad irresponsible Muslims. Are we naming and shaming the wrong people?

6.  The complete lack of common sense on the part of some of our leaders is a cause for concern. If there are two groups at odds with one another, you don't sit down with just one and then declare their grievances are justified. Nor do you express sympathy for someone who's been responsible for many violent deaths and say that you could have

rehabilitated them. Even sillier, you don't try to equate the 'pain' a chair might feel upon being whipped with what a human being might feel.

7. While some leaders talk about eliminating corruption, most remain blind to obvious questions, such as, how come a public official can afford a RM25 million mansion? No wonder cynicism reigns!

8. The increasing racist tone by which we refer to foreigners within our midst, especially those who are from countries less developed than ours. Racist monikers may not be OK for our own people but apparently OK for others. Also despicable are the sweeping generalisations about foreigners as criminals, conmen and prostitutes.

9. The constant politicisation of everything. Really, neither politics nor politicians are the most important things in the world.

Things I Have Been Happy About:

10. The increase in the number of people who have become more aware of the issues surrounding them and are keen to express their opinions, mostly online.

11. The many young people who are not only increasingly aware of issues around them but will also take action to effect some change. The most impressive is the

MyConstitution campaign to educate the public about our 'Document of Destiny' but also other smaller projects such as Fast for the Nation which does more for unity than any government project could.

12. The effectiveness of social media especially Facebook and Twitter in connecting like-minded people so that they can share experiences, learn from one another and get organised. As always young people are way ahead of adults, especially those in government.

13. The fact that we can talk about human rights without the ground opening up and swallowing us.

14. The continued belief in this country, despite all the nastiness, and the willingness to stay and fight.

There's probably more I could be happy about if I thought hard enough but the horrid things somehow come quicker to mind.

Whatever comes along, things must get better in 2010. Wish you all a Merry Christmas and a Happy Muslim and Gregorian New Year!

*23 December 2009*

---

* Kartika Sari Dewi Shukarno was sentenced to whipping and a RM5000 fine by the Pahang Shariah Court for drinking beer. Her sentence was later reduced to community service.

# Resolutions for One and All

It's the New Year and, as with convention, we should really make resolutions, even though the chances of keeping them are slim. I get more half-hearted about making them each year although my list nowadays tends to be short and realistic, with a 50% chance of being kept.

I do, however, like to indulge in making lists for other people. For my children, I wish they would resolve to work harder at school and be tidier. For my colleagues and friends, I wish that they (and I) could brush aside small problems and concentrate on the big ones.

Needless to say, I can't help but wish for resolutions from our various public figures, particularly those in Government. Here's a list of some, in no particular order.

I wish that our Government would resolve to:

1. Slap down rather than merely slap the wrists of those public figures and politicians who misbehave. Just say 'that's nonsense and we won't stand for it!' rather than the wishy-washy 'we must investigate' reaction. Or worse still, complete silence.

2. Stop twisting words around in order to spin what's wrong into what's right.

3.  Stop using simpering journalists to interview politicians because they do a great job of convincing the public that both they and their interviewees are nothing but idiots.

4.  Stop demonising people who are critical and calling them traitors when they probably love their country more than most.

5.  Stop being afraid of those who think that getting ahead means getting handouts for everything in the belief that this will let them stand tall.

6.  Do the right thing even when it may make them unpopular for a while. Ban plastic bags. Push for safer sex. Outlaw child marriages.

7.  Remind some people that they are paid by taxpayers to do their jobs and that does not entitle them to act as if they are God's representatives on earth.

8.  In fact, I truly wish we could just forget about having to use taxpayers' money to pay anyone who is likely to believe they are God's representatives on earth.

9.  Allow more consultation with people on the ground who know what communities need for their own development. Maybe have a policy that ensures that absolutely nobody is marginalised for any reason.

10. Overhaul the entire education system to make it more open, democratic, and on par with the best in the world. And completely eradicate politics from it.

11. Make sports and the arts as important as economic development because we need to have a country with soul.

12. Ban the habit of giving titles to sports, arts and entertainment figures until they're at least 50 or have had significant achievements in their field for a number of years. Roger Federer has been No. 1 in the tennis world for a record-breaking 237 weeks and the Swiss government still hasn't made him a datuk.

I wish politicians would resolve to

1. Stop politicking and concede that sometimes the other side can be right.

2. Work together more on issues that affect everyone. Australia's successful HIV programme worked well because from the very beginning, the government and opposition decided it was a bipartisan issue.

3. Be more self-reflective. And breath before they say anything.

4. Get rid of sexism everywhere it is found, especially in political parties, in Parliament and State Assemblies and

in general commentary.

5.  Come out and unequivocally condemn violence against women, no ifs, no buts.

6.  Publicly shake the hand of a HIV-positive adult.

I wish the police would resolve to:

1.  Ticket every single person who double- and triple-parks on Fridays and not excuse them just because they are apparently communing with God. Or, watching football.

2.  Stop finding parangs in the cars of every single person who accuses them of wrongdoing.

3.  Stop shrugging their shoulders every time someone complains of their bags being snatched, laptops stolen, etc. Police reports aren't just for claiming insurance or getting new ICs done.

I wish Malaysians in general would:

1.  Use their car signal lights for a change.

2.  Queue.

3.  Park in the right places, dead straight and not encroach onto empty spots.

4.  Not double and triple-park in front of mosques on Fridays and think that God is OK with it.

5.  Stop waiting for someone else to do something.

6.  Stop putting down people who do do something.

7.  Stop reading so much gossip and trash. It really doesn't reflect well on us.

8.  Stop believing everything they read. Just because it's on the Internet really doesn't make it truer.

9.  Register to vote if they haven't yet.

10. Remember that their votes are valuable and should not be given away on empty promises.

Happy 2011, folks!

*10 January 2011*

# How to Win an Argument in Malaysia

In light of recent events and with the lack of guidance from up top on how to conduct ourselves in an argument, I thought I would volunteer some tips on How to Win an Argument in Malaysia.

1. Decide what stance you want to take on something. It doesn't have to be based on facts or logic, just what you felt when you woke up this morning, especially if you got up on the wrong side of the bed.

2. Don't consult anyone on the facts of the matter. What matters is how you feel about it. The grumpier it makes you feel, the better.

3. I take that back. Do consult your boss about it. If he looks doubtful, persuade him that he doesn't have to do the arguing, you will do it. It'll make him look serene, if somewhat vacant.

4. Pick on a target. Ensure that they are people who are unlikely to be able to fight back. The best targets are those whom most of us would never have noticed until you point them out. This is what makes you a pioneer.

5. Fire the first salvo and make sure the media hears it. Don't

write it down, just shout it out. If the media look blank, it's only because they don't understand what you're saying. If anyone says you don't make sense, it's only because their brains are in the wrong place.

6. Watch the ensuing hoohah. With glee.

7. If anyone says you don't know the law, ignore it. You are not concerned with the laws of mere earthlings. Even though occasionally you do aspire to be an earthling lawmaker.

8. Get your mates to shout out variations of the same thing you just said. This will make it sound as if a lot of people agree on the same thing. They don't have to sound nice and polite. That's for wimps.

9. While you're at it, take a swipe at any other group that has the temerity to look askance at what you say. Women, for example. Women really should just shut up and put out. Whatever did we give them the vote for?

10. Meanwhile, assure the boss that everything's being taken care of. The media and everyone's talking about it every day. You could never get this many column inches by doing the same old same old make nice stuff.

11. If anyone has the cheek to say you're talking nonsense and are not worth commenting on, try and act as if you don't

care. But make sure the media knows what you think about it when you don't care.

12. If the public thinks other people make more sense than you, tell them they are confused. Confused is what everyone else is. You, on the other hand, are crystal clear. They are wrong.

13. Make sure none of the voices that sound different from you get heard. Who needs such cacophony anyway? Yours is the only harmonious one there is. So make sure that the papers and TV only air your views. They need to sell anyway, the poor things.

14. Never enter into a debate except through statements in the media. And try not to get on the liberal colonial-language media, even the one owned by Arabs. That was a muff-up, sending that young fellow who doesn't speak very well to that TV station. Who knew they'd send some slick smooth-talking chap up against him?

15. Grand media gestures, especially if they're TV-friendly, are the way to go. Those bum-shaking dudes a few years ago were really inspiring.

16. If anyone outside the country dares to complain about what you're saying, tell them to butt out. This is Malaysia. We are different. Never mind if we still want to have the same mobile phones, TVs, handbags and cars as anyone

else in the world. Get it right, we are different.

17. That doesn't mean that anyone within the country is allowed to be different though. No way. How to have harmony if everyone is different? No, we must all be on, how do you say it, the same sheet! In fact if we can all look the same, even better. But we'll start with thinking the same first.

18. If our foreign brethren start saying that we haven't got it right, ignore them. They may be able to read our holy texts like they're reading the newspaper but that doesn't mean they know anything. Why don't they just stick to getting oil out of the ground and leave us alone?

19. And those foreign brethren who are laughing at us, obviously they're colonial stooges and have breathed the air in the West for so long, it's gone to their heads. It's Malaysian haze they should all be breathing! Why do you think our brains work this way?

20. History? Who cares about history? We are making history, by being the first country to create problems where none exist. Who else can claim that?

Happy arguing!

*18 January 2014*

# Glossary

**ADUN** Ahli Dewan Undangan Negeri (Member of the State Legislative Assembly). Representatives are elected from each constituency during state-level elections.

**Al-Fatihah** A name for the first chapter or surah of the Qur'an. The main literal translation of the expression is 'The Opening'.

**azan** Muslim call to ritual prayer.

**Bersih** The short name for the Coalition for Free and Fair Elections (Gabungan Pilihanraya Bersih dan Adil) in Malaysia. It also means 'clean' in Malay.

**BR1M** 1 Malaysia People's Aid (Bantuan Rakyat 1 Malaysia), a government aid scheme to assist low-income families and individuals against rising living costs.

*buka puasa* Malay term, literally meaning 'breaking of fast', which refers to the evening meal at which Muslims break their Ramadan fast.

*ceramah* Malay for 'lecture', but often with the additional connotation of a political rally.

*gotong royong* A Malaysian cultural practice centred around mutual assistance and communal cooperation.

**GST** Goods and services tax, introduced in 2015.

**IGP** Inspector-General of Police – heads the Royal Malaysia Police Force.

**ISIS (IS)** Islamic State of Iraq and the Levant. An extremist terrorist group based in Syria and Iraq, with global affiliates.

**JAKIM** Jabatan Kemajuan Islam Malaysia (Department of Islamic Development

Malaysia), responsible for developing Islam in Malaysia.

**JAWI**   Jabatan Agama Islam Wilayah Persekutuan (Department of Federal Territory Islamic Affairs), leads Islamic administration in the Federal Territories of Kuala Lumpur, Labuan and Putrajaya.

**JPJ**   Jabatan Pengangkutan Jalan Malaysia (Malaysian Road Transport Department), responsible for regulation and enforcement of certain transport-related activities such as registering drivers and vehicles, road safety, etc.

**Kaaba**   The holiest site in Islam, located in Mecca, Saudi Arabia.

**k-economy**   Knowledge-based economy. Malaysia is seeking to transition from a production-based economy to a k-economy.

*khalwat*   Close proximity.

Under Malaysia's Islamic (shariah) laws, unmarried Muslims who meet persons of the opposite gender in private can be charged with this offense.

**KL**   Abbreviation for Kuala Lumpur.

**KLIA**   Abbreviation for Kuala Lumpur International Airport.

*kuih*   Malay cakes or snacks.

**LGBT**   Lesbian-Gay-Bisexual-Transgender.

**Selamat Hari Raya,** *maaf zahir batin*   The common greeting during the Hari Raya Aidilfitri, or Eid season; the latter three words mean 'forgive my physical or emotional wrongdoings'.

**markas**   Election offices that are active during campaigns. Each political party will set up a markas.

**Masjid Negara**   Malaysia's national mosque, located in Kuala Lumpur.

*mat rempit*s   Term used for

male motorbike-riding youths, many of whom participate in illegal street motorbike racing, gangtersism and violent crime.

*mat salleh*  A colloquial term used to describe Caucasians.

*merdeka*  A Malay word that means 'freedom' or 'independence'.

*mufti*  An Islamic legal expert.

*nasi biryani*  A popular rice dish made with meat, egg, vegetables and several spices.

*niat*  As Islamic concept regarding one's intent before performing an action.

**Pasar Ramadan**  Outdoor bazaar selling food and drinks during Ramadan, where many go to break their fast.

**pbuh**  Peace be upon him. A phrase that follows the name of any prophet or angel in Islam as a sign of respect.

*sahur*  The pre-dawn meal consumed by Muslims before fasting after sunrise during Ramadan.

**salam**  Arabic for 'peace'.

**Shawwal**  The 10th month of the Islamic calendar.

**SMS**  Short message service, a text message sent or received via mobile phones using this service.

*tudung*  Headscarf worn by Malay women.

**Tumblr**  A microblogging platform and social networking website.

*ugama*  Islamic religion.

*ulama*  Muslim scholars or religious leaders.

*ustazah*  Title given to a female Islamic teacher.

**Wanita**  Malay word for woman. Most Malaysian political parties have a Wanita branch.

**YB**  Yang Berhormat. Malay for 'the honourable'. Style accorded to members of Malaysia's Parliament and State Legislative Assemblies.